# 'Whole-Brain' Behaviour Management in the Classroom

*'Whole-Brain' Behaviour Management in the Classroom* represents a brave and insightful shift away from narrow perspectives on behaviour management and draws practitioners towards a more holistic understanding of ourselves and how we impact on children's learning and behaviour.

The authors' brilliant new conceptual model of 'whole-brain' behaviour management acknowledges each practitioner's own unique profile of strengths as well as areas for development. Their pioneering 'whole-brain' approach draws upon a range of influences and concepts that cross discipline boundaries, expanding on the practitioner's understanding of the complexity of children's behaviour through their own knowledge of neuroscience, biopsychosocial theory and interpersonal awareness.

The book will take the reader through a process of self-evaluation in which their preferred ways of thinking, acting and relating will be explored and interpreted in order to help them understand their 'personal style' and how it impacts on the children in their care. In reading this book you will:

* explore the spectrum of competencies required for effective behaviour management;
* analyse and reflect deeply on your own beliefs, feelings and behaviour;
* recognise that habitual ways of thinking, feelings and acting in the classroom can change;
* gain a thorough understanding of the complexity of behaviour management by engaging with realistic case studies;
* develop greater personal responsibility for managing behaviour and establishing and maintaining harmonious working relationships in the classroom.

Offering new insights and creative solutions, this is an essentially practical guide to coach practitioners in their personal and professional development, helping them to raise the achievement of children exhibiting even the most challenging of behaviour.

**Chris Derrington** was previously the head of a school for children with emotional and behavioural difficulties, and is currently Senior Lecturer in Inclusive Education at the University of Northampton.

**Hilary Goddard** is in her third headship.

# 'Whole-Brain' Behaviour Management in the Classroom

## Every Piece of the Puzzle

Chris Derrington and
Hilary Goddard

Routledge
Taylor & Francis Group

LONDON AND NEW YORK

First published 2008
by Routledge
2 Park Square, Milton Park, Abingdon, Oxon OX14 4RN

Simultaneously published in the USA and Canada
by Routledge
270 Madison Ave, New York, NY 10016

*Routledge is an imprint of the Taylor & Francis Group, an informa business*

Typeset in Garamond3 by
RefineCatch Limited, Bungay, Suffolk
Printed and bound in Great Britain by
TJ International Ltd, Padstow, Cornwall

*British Library Cataloguing in Publication Data*
A catalogue record for this book is available from the British Library

*Library of Congress Cataloging in Publication Data*
Library of Congress Cataloging-in-Publication Data
Derrington, Chris
"Whole-brain" behaviour management in the classroom: every
piece of the puzzle / Chris Derrington and Hilary Goddard.
p. cm.
Includes bibliographical references.
1. Classroom management—Study and teaching. 2. Behaviour
modification. 3. Teacher effectiveness. I. Goddard, Hilary, 1956–
II. Title.
LB3013.D47 2007
371.102′4—dc22
2007013948

ISBN10: 0–415–41180–7 (hbk)
ISBN10: 0–415–41181–5 (pbk)
ISBN10: 0–203–93437–7 (ebk)

ISBN13: 978–0–415–41180–6 (hbk)
ISBN13: 978–0–415–41181–3 (pbk)
ISBN13: 978–0–203–93437–1 (ebk)

# Contents

# Figures

# Tables

# Acknowledgements

We would like to thank: John, Mike, Tom, David, Amy, Bryony and Joe for their supreme patience with us; the amazing staff of Ramridge Primary School for their receptiveness, resilience, responsibility and resolute optimism; Class B, who started us off on this long journey and whose names we borrowed for our fictional teachers; and finally all the children and teachers we have been lucky enough to work with and who taught us everything we know.

Hilary Goddard and Chris Derrington

## About the authors

Between them, Chris Derrington and Hilary Goddard have 45 years' experience of teaching pupils with behavioural, emotional and social difficulties in mainstream and special schools. Hilary is currently the head teacher of Ramridge Primary School in Luton and has acknowledged success in bringing three primary schools out of serious weaknesses. Chris has been the head teacher of a school for pupils with serious behavioural difficulties and is currently a senior lecturer in the School of Education at the University of Northampton.

# Part I

# Blue sky thinking

# Chapter 1

# Opening the box

If the only tool you have is a hammer, you tend to see every problem as a nail.

(Abraham Maslow, 1908–1970[1])

## Introduction

This well-known quotation is generally attributed to Abraham Maslow, the eminent humanistic psychologist. Allegedly, he coined this popular maxim in the 1960s as part of a comment about the limitations of behaviourism in psychological research, but it has since been adopted widely by initiators of change in just about every professional field. What the saying suggests is that there is a universal tendency for individuals to rely upon a familiar 'tool' for solving a range of problems even though this tool may be ineffective at times or even unfit for purpose. A 'tool' in this context is any kind of response used to tackle a problem and is usually driven by a particular belief or perception about the problem itself.

Let's think about this in terms of behaviour management and consider three hypothetical teachers. The first teacher tends to use the tool of 'tactical ignoring' on a frequent basis, and this is grounded in her perception that when students misbehave in class there is a conscious intention on their part to divert and steal her attention away from other, more deserving students. Although she may not be consciously aware of it, her inner belief is that disruptive students do not deserve to win attention in this way and, as far as she is concerned, she won't give in to it. Her response is to punish the students concerned by denying them the attention they crave. The second teacher regularly yells at students when their behaviour irritates her. The type of behaviour that provokes the shouting can range from forgetting to bring a pen or producing untidy work through to deliberate non-compliance. This teacher defends her style of behaviour management by maintaining that students can easily become out of control and that they need to be kept in their place and understand that teachers hold the balance of power. The third teacher often threatens his lively class with the intervention of a senior colleague because he believes deep down that he himself lacks the authority and credibility to manage the students' behaviour as effectively as his colleague.

Although their favourite tools might be entirely appropriate in some instances (for example a loud shout could prevent a fight from breaking out) these three teachers continue to adopt and depend on these strategies even though the tactical ignoring often results in an escalation of the unwanted behaviour, the shouting usually evokes equally hostile responses and aggressive challenges from some of the students, and the senior colleague is usually too busy or disinclined to intervene in the third class. In each case, the teacher's repertoire for managing student behaviour has become self-limiting. To avoid the limitations of any one tool, every teacher, like any other professional, needs to have many at his/her disposal. This advice sounds easy enough, so why do these teachers continue to limit their responses in this way?

According to the concept of 'Maslow's hammer', what happens is that we unconsciously distort our perception of events around us and become ever more selective in what we choose to focus on, so that our preferred 'hammer' always appears to be the most appropriate tool there is. In the case of the second teacher, the student who forgets to bring a pen to class is perceived as having done this deliberately to challenge the teacher's authority and test her patience. The problem behaviour (in this case, forgetting to bring a pen) is habitually perceived as a 'nail' (the challenging of her authority) that therefore needs to be 'hammered' (the teacher yells to restore her authority). If the outcome of our action is unsatisfactory, because the initial problem wasn't a nail after all, we experience cognitive dissonance and, to cope with this, we protect our internal representations and our belief-driven behaviour by placing the blame elsewhere. Blaming is what we do when we are unwilling or feel unable to take restorative action ourselves and this can include the search for better, alternative solutions.

It is not easy to change the beliefs and perceptions we hold about others and ourselves or to adopt new ways of thinking, feeling and behaving and, because behaviour management is an emotive and sensitive issue, teachers often feel too embarrassed or even ashamed to talk openly about their experiences. Simply being told what you should say and do by a senior colleague or manager is unlikely to initiate long-lasting change and may even lead to more anxiety and a further reduction in effectiveness, particularly if this advice is linked to competency procedures. Training events led by charismatic behaviour consultants may be highly entertaining and inspirational but they can leave some teachers feeling inadequate because they could never, in a million years, imagine themselves being able to exude such 'personality capital', confidence and prowess when dealing with challenging behaviour. Although whole-school intervention approaches such as assertive discipline (Canter and Canter, 1992) have been embraced enthusiastically by a number of schools in the UK, there is still limited empirical evidence to support their long-term effectiveness (Evans *et al.*, 2003), and it has also been acknowledged that inconsistency in interpretation, application and delivery by different teachers impedes their effectiveness (Fox, 1991; Taylor, 2003).

We believe there is a need for a radically different and tailored approach to behaviour management training, one that encourages teachers to develop their self-knowledge or intrapersonal intelligence (Gardner, 1993) and helps them to realise that they have the inner resources to alter their perceptions and thus expand the range of tools they have at their disposal. Reflective practice has its roots in the writings of John Dewey (1916), who described life as an experiential journey made up of problems for us to solve. Dewey suggested that we could achieve this by taking a step back and viewing the situation holistically before taking subsequent action. This also has links with 'double-loop' learning (Argyris, 1976) in which assumptions underlying one's current views are questioned and tested out. By applying these principles, teachers may become better equipped to manage the challenges that present themselves on a day-to-day basis.

Most books on classroom behaviour management are written for teachers but are mainly about children or young people and how to deal with them. This book represents a shift in approach. Firstly, it is about teachers rather than students. Secondly, it challenges the supposition that teachers are a homogeneous group with identical training needs. 'Whole-brain' behaviour management (WBBM) highlights the individual teacher as a key variable in successful behaviour management and recognises that his/her internal model of reality including perceptions, beliefs and feelings all impact on relationships and management skills in the classroom. Scripts and learned techniques can help to improve behaviour management up to a point but become superficial and virtually useless if applied without authenticity and congruence with what the teacher believes and feels within.

From a social constructivist perspective, this book does not attempt to provide the answers as we see them (through our view of the truth). Rather than offering yet more tips on how to manage behaviour, we intend to provide a broad theoretical framework within which teachers are encouraged to acknowledge, reflect upon and analyse what they already feel, think, say and do. It is an existential process that assists us to make sense of our world.

This book contains many opportunities for guided self-reflection through the presentation of authentic case studies, exercises and self-audits, all designed to promote critical analysis. Essentially, the book is a personal guide that will coach and support individual teachers in initiating change and ultimately achieving a more balanced set of personal and professional competencies. It is our hope that the 'whole-brain' approach will offer some fresh new insights and creative solutions to behaviour management and help all teachers to recognise the link between their personal constructs[2] (the way they construe the world) and their responses to behaviour in the classroom. In doing this, teachers will feel greater ownership of outcomes and become more energised and more able to reclaim their personal empowerment and avoid giving it away to others (Zull, 2002). Fundamentally, this book, which draws on a converging synthesis of emerging research in the fields of cognitive neuroscience and positive psychology with ancient theories and existential Eastern philosophies, is about discovery, self-knowledge and the nature of human relationships.

This book will help teachers to:

- explore the spectrum of competencies required for effective behaviour management;
- analyse and reflect deeply upon their own beliefs, feelings and behaviour;
- gain a thorough understanding of the complexity of behaviour management by engaging with realistic case studies;

- identify what changes they can make in themselves and plan a course of action;
- develop greater personal responsibility for managing behaviour and establishing and maintaining harmonious working relationships in the classroom.

## How we came to develop 'whole-brain' behaviour management

For the past five years we have been formulating our theory of 'whole-brain' behaviour management, but our journey began much earlier than this. Our paths first crossed as young teachers in 1982 when we shared the teaching of a class of children with severe behavioural, emotional and social difficulties in a residential special school, as we alternately took periods of maternity leave and expanded our own families with faultless synchronicity! During the twenty years that followed, our careers took separate paths and between us we taught and managed in a wide range of educational provision including other special schools and units for students with behavioural difficulties, mainstream primary and secondary schools, and local authority services, as well as inspecting schools and conducting educational research.

Despite the geographical distance between us, we remained in contact with each other and around the time that we experienced (separately) the stark reality of taking up our first headship roles in very challenging schools we began to meet up occasionally at a very nice health spa to help us unwind and recharge our batteries! Inevitably, we also used these opportunities to offload our concerns, discuss educational matters and generally 'put the world to rights'. Soon, our regular discussions developed into quite animated and lengthy debates that explored our shared (and sometimes conflicting) interests in psychology, neuroscience, philosophy and spirituality. We had both rediscovered the psychological and philosophical works of William James, written more than a hundred years ago but eerily prophetic in his description of cutting-edge research in the field of cognitive neuroscience. We were also both interested in the Portuguese neuroscientist Antonio Damasio's theory of emotion, which challenges the ideology that cognition is a separate entity from emotion. When we began to really analyse our ideas about student behaviour and its management, we realised the extent of our alignment after all those years and, energised by this, we began to write our thoughts down and even fill notebooks during our spa visits. Rather like Archimedes, everything became clear in the jacuzzi, and the 'whole-brain' model began to surface!

Historically, behaviour management models have reflected socio-political developments in how children are perceived and valued. For example, in Victorian Britain, the mantra of 'children being seen and not heard' manifested itself in a physically punitive and restrictive behaviour regime, whereas the progressive culture of the 1960s and 1970s led to a challenge of authoritarianism, a growth in child-centred practices and a far more permissive classroom environment. Our overall concern is that the prevailing social climate in the UK has become characterised by a universal paranoia of youth culture in which young people are routinely scapegoated as 'yobs' and 'thugs', alienated, demonised and even criminalised through a growing mistrust fuelled by media hype and scaremongering. It seemed to us that this negative representation was beginning to generate a climate of social fear that was permeating all levels of society (including schools) and creating a growing divide between 'them' (children and young people) and 'us' (the adults).

The increasing number of children being prescribed 'class A' drugs such as Ritalin[3] to enable them to be tolerated in the mainstream classroom, the abundance of sensationalist reality TV programmes revelling in 'shocking' antics of children and teenagers, the social exclusion of youths for wearing a hooded garment,[4] the proliferation of anti-social behaviour orders (ASBOs)[5] served on juveniles, and references to 'feral' children in the popular press all contribute to the growing rhetoric that makes us question our capacity to tackle and stem the 'rising tide'. This attitude persists even though national crime figures and school inspection reports provide evidence to negate the assumption that standards of behaviour are worsening. This pervading sense of helplessness goes hand in hand with the illegality of corporal punishment, which in an earlier age was used to 'control' the child. Current legislation, introduced to promote respect and greater community cohesion, seems to focus more on the enforcement of zero tolerance and punitive short-term measures than on enduring and preventive ones. Such an approach makes no distinction between equal and equitable treatment and also fails to acknowledge the ways in which inflexible and limiting social structures, systems and educational policy can lie at the root of disaffection and anti-social behaviour. This increasing disconnection between young people and adults has reached the point where anti-social behaviour amongst British teenagers is reportedly now the worst in Europe (Margo *et al.*, 2006).

Within our professional roles, we have noticed too how colleagues and peers are ever more intent on finding the key to better behaviour in classrooms. Policy makers search for a common approach or framework that can be applied to every school in their area, providing a level of co-ordination that central government requires of them. Head teachers and special educational needs co-ordinators eagerly subscribe to any new resource materials or packaged approaches that come on to the market promising to make a positive impact on student behaviour. Everyone is looking for the missing piece that will solve the puzzle of behaviour management. The problem is, everybody's jigsaw is unique and so we all need to find different missing pieces!

## What do we mean by 'whole-brain' behaviour management?

In order to explain what 'whole-brain' behaviour management (WBBM) is, it is important to begin by clarifying what it is not! 'Whole-brain' behaviour management is not a pseudo-scientific fad or some gimmicky intervention based on over-simplified theories of hemispheric dominance (left- and right-brain thinking) or learning styles. Neither is it a quick-fix approach that promises to solve behaviour management problems overnight with tips and tricks for securing student compliance. Classroom behaviour is such a complex phenomenon that it can't possibly be addressed in such simplistic ways.

Unlike some other approaches that seem to focus on 'problem behaviour' as something belonging to the child and needing to be remedied by an external intervention of some kind or another (like a first-aid model), the WBBM approach is centred firmly on the thoughts, feelings and behaviour of teachers. Many teachers today are fully aware of the techniques and strategies associated with assertive and positive behaviour management but still experience relational difficulties, stress, anxiety and even conflict in the classroom. This may be because they lack the confidence or belief in themselves to carry out the strategies with conviction; perhaps they just find it hard to break old habits and ways of working; maybe they are loath to consider alternative methods or perhaps they are threatened by a relationship-based approach that makes them feel vulnerable in the classroom. Some teachers carry emotional baggage of their own which makes it difficult for them to feel energised, to act empathetically or to be able to expose their human qualities. Other teachers may already be outstandingly good communicators but because they lack particular aspects of pedagogical knowledge or psychological awareness or organisational skills this, in turn, impacts negatively on classroom behaviour.

Trends in behaviour management training that claim to equip teachers with top tips or winning scripts that can somehow be bolted on to everybody's existing practice often fail to take account of this diversity (the profile of the individual teacher) as well as overlooking the complexity of children's and young people's social, emotional and psychological needs. As a result, the strategies that they promote are rarely suitable for all teachers or sustainable over time. These simplistic approaches are essentially behaviourist in origin and are based on the assumption that human beings can be moulded by external factors. Such approaches are also limited by the Western notion of psychology and psychiatry: that a rational model can explain all human behaviour. Other more recent developments in the area of emotional literacy (for example Sharp, 2001; Weare, 2004) represent an important shift in thinking and practice, but still contribute only part of what is required to manage behaviour effectively.

Like the three teachers outlined at the beginning of this chapter, we can easily become stuck in a groove where particular thought patterns, beliefs and behaviour become habitual responses even though they always seem to lead to the same unsatisfactory outcomes. This can lead to a lowering of teacher morale and job satisfaction. It is important to re-emphasise that most of what we 'see' in the external world is a function of our internal assumptions and beliefs; we tend to see and interpret the world as we have always seen and interpreted it (habitual patterns). We perceptually ignore or filter out a plethora of alternative possibilities or multiple realities that could otherwise help to explain events. A study by Miller *et al.* (2000) for example found that the attributions by students for misbehaviour in school were markedly different to those held by teachers. If we accept that our own internal assumptions and beliefs are responsible for the way that we attribute our own and other people's behaviour and, consciously or not, we convey these expectations in our daily interactions then it stands to reason that what we expect is what we get! Teachers who hold (and therefore communicate) high expectations of their students in terms of achievement and behaviour generally obtain better results than those who expect the opposite.

Just as children and young people are individuals with their own dispositions, skills, characteristics and distinct ways of thinking, feeling and responding in the classroom, so too are the adults who teach and support them in their learning. Although they may share certain insecurities and vulnerabilities in relation to behaviour management, teachers are unique individuals each with their own life experiences, strengths and personal challenges. What we are implying here is that, if teachers are to become more accomplished in all aspects of behaviour management, they are going to require a flexible and differentiated approach to their training and professional development. We are suggesting that this can best be achieved through the enhancement of metacognitive awareness (see also Chapter 4).

Metacognition (first described by Flavell, 1976) is the conscious awareness of our own knowledge and the ability to understand, control and manipulate our own cognitive processes. In short, metacognition is the ability to recognise and analyse the thoughts and personal constructs that shape our behaviour. It allows us to understand that we have a selection of appropriate tools, strategies and inner resources at our disposal to help us move forward and enables us to regulate and evaluate our on-going progress in an objective way.

Metacognition can help teachers to become more effective practitioners in the management of behaviour by:

- encouraging them to cultivate a higher level of critical thinking which strengthens their self-awareness;
- encouraging them to take responsibility for analysing and adapting their thinking;
- encouraging them to assume conscious control of their own personal and professional development.

Although self-talk and introspection are central features of this metacognitive approach, WBBM also recognises that peer coaching can provide an excellent vehicle for teachers to talk to another professional about these thought processes without being judged or appraised. In fact, it is often in the process of formulating one's thoughts in order to express them to others that metacognition is enhanced, leading to change (Freire, 1996). Advice about using peer coaching as part of the model is provided in Chapter 5.

To sum up so far: in coining the phrase ' "whole-brain" behaviour management' we are referring to a holistic, developmental process, with an enabling philosophy that focuses on teachers' individual needs and circumstances. It encourages teachers to make connections, to think paradoxically, to harmonise their thoughts, feelings and behaviour and to consider radical ways of perceiving events and relating to others, by drawing upon their emotional, rational, intellectual, spiritual and creative resources. It is not a quick-fix approach but a long-term process during which perceptions and beliefs may be scrutinised, challenged and transformed in the search for fulfilment, balance and greater job satisfaction. The sub-title of this book, 'Every Piece of the Puzzle', acknowledges the enigmatic nature of behaviour and the need to be aware of the complexity of factors that affect our capacity to manage it effectively. It also highlights the fact that, in terms of a conceptual model, 'whole-brain' behaviour management draws upon and makes connections between diverse disciplinary influences (see Chapter 3).

The key spheres of influence include recent discoveries and research in the field of cognitive and affective neuroscience, the emerging school of positive psychology, and links with ancient philosophical wisdom and esoteric spiritual practices. This synthesis of theory provides a unifying framework and resonates with what a number of commentators are beginning to refer to as a systemic or holistic paradigm shift (for example Ferguson, 1980, 2002; Gerhardt, 2004). A paradigm (derived from the Greek *paradigma*, meaning pattern) is a conceptual framework or a scheme for understanding reality. A paradigm shift (a term coined by Thomas Kuhn in 1962) is a distinctly new worldview or way of thinking about phenomena that ultimately leads to a cultural transformation. For example, the scientific discoveries of Sir Isaac Newton dramatically changed our perspective on the nature of the physical world and our place in it, until this was superseded by another paradigm shift caused by Einstein's theory of relativity. In the last years of his life, Maslow began to work on what he termed the 'fourth force' in psychology (following on from psychodynamic theory, behaviourism and his own humanistic perspective). Maslow's fourth force was coined 'transpersonal psychology' (beyond the personal) and is concerned with the processes by which individuals experience a deeper or wider sense of who they are and a sense of greater connectedness with others and their environment (Maslow, 1968). Maslow's fourth force drew upon Eastern philosophies and investigated the concept of higher levels of consciousness, including aspects of meditation. It is important to emphasise that the transpersonal branch of psychology is an academic discipline and not a religious or New Age spiritual movement.

For those readers who are interested in understanding more about the theoretical framework that shaped the model, these influences and their connections are more fully explored in the next two chapters. Other readers may prefer to pass over these for the time being and learn more immediately about how the model itself might work for them.

---

### Key principles of 'whole-brain' behaviour management

- Behaviour management is complex and never simplistic.
- Quick-fix solutions are rarely sustainable over time.
- Teachers are a heterogeneous group – one size does not fit all and we all need to work on different things.
- Subjective reality drives beliefs.
- If we keep doing things in the same way, we will keep getting the same outcomes.
- An 'objective' self-perception is the first step to effective personal and professional development.

---

## What the book contains

We are not suggesting that you read this book from cover to cover or work systematically through the chapters in the order in which they are presented. Just as with any other guidebook, we anticipate that some readers will prefer to dip in and out of it and others will be drawn to certain chapters that they immediately identify with. Those readers who are interested in learning more about the theoretical context that helped to shape this book might want to look first at Chapter 2, which explores existing and emerging theories of the brain and its workings, while Chapter 3 details the interdisciplinary framework that underpins the 'whole-brain' approach.

Chapter 4 contains a self-reporting instrument to help practitioners identify their self-perceptions and preferred ways of thinking, feeling and behaving. This instrument is used to identify the teacher's CAB (cognitive, affective and behavioural) profile and will help teachers to audit and prioritise the aspects of behaviour management that they may want to address first. The concept of 'whole-brain' behaviour management is represented by a visual model introduced in Chapter 5. This model identifies six broad domains for effective behaviour management which, together, make up a wheel of competencies. Each domain is further subdivided into six components devised to help teachers reflect more specifically on particular elements of their classroom management.

---

### Key domains for effective behaviour management

- Psychology (Chapter 6)
- Knowledge (Chapter 7)
- Organisation (Chapter 8)
- Communication (Chapter 9)
- Emotional literacy (Chapter 10)
- Self-efficacy (Chapter 11)

---

In the second part of the book (Chapters 6–11) readers are introduced to six fictional teachers. Each of these chapters focuses on one of the teachers introduced below, describing and analysing their experiences and responses in an interactive way while illustrating their profile of competencies in managing behaviour. The teachers are caricatures, but we have drawn upon our professional experience to try to make them as 'real' and believable as possible.

---

- Belinda: an experienced teacher who works in a specialist unit for students who have been excluded from mainstream school
- Adrian: a recently qualified primary school teacher
- Hayley: a modern foreign languages teacher in a secondary school

- Douglas: a tutor in motor mechanics at a college of further education
- Sabia: head of the ICT department in a secondary school
- Trevor: a primary school teacher

Chapter 12 reflects on the power of synergy (with references to gestalt psychology and systems theory) and explains why this lies at the heart of the WBBM model.

# Chapter 2

# Laying the pieces out

> The power of attention not only allows us to choose what mental direction we will take. It also allows us . . . to change – in scientifically demonstrable ways – the systematic functioning of our own neural circuitry.
>
> (Schwartz and Begley, 2002: 366)

In the United States, the 1990s were designated 'The Decade of the Brain' by an Act of Congress. This initiative led to a proliferation of neuroscientific (brain) research studies, and consequently a number of important discoveries have been made in recent years about the anatomy, function and circuitry of the brain.

One of the outcomes of this development is that cognitive neuroscientific research findings have promoted a heightened interest amongst educationists (Hall, 2005). For example, the term 'wholebrain' has begun to surface in educational circles to describe particular teaching interventions or approaches that are based on notions of preferred learning styles or which claim to balance or integrate 'right-brain' and 'left-brain' thinking. While such teaching methods may have a certain value, it has been observed by a number of independent neuroscientists that the claims made by some of these are, at best, based on a shaky foundation (Bruer, 1997; Coffield *et al.*, 2004; Geake, 2005; Goswami, 2004). For example, popular assumptions about hemispheric laterality (often referred to as left-brain/right-brain) are based on a 'gross simplification' which is no longer supported by modern neuroscientific research (Bruer, 1999; OECD, 2002). Furthermore, as Hargreaves (2005: 11) warns, 'In misguided hands, learning styles could become not a means of personalizing learning but a new version of general intelligence that slots learners into preconceived categories and puts unwarranted ceilings on their intellectual development and achievement.' These are important caveats that teachers need to be aware of.

In business studies and industry, 'whole-brain' models such as Herrmann's dominant thinking model (1990) are increasingly being used to analyse and understand how managers and employees think and make decisions and how they communicate. Herrmann's model is based on a metaphoric representation of the brain that is divided into four quadrants of cognitive preferences (cerebral pairs and limbic pairs; see Figure 2.1) and is designed to help individuals to act outside of their preferred thinking preferences and enhance their overall effectiveness. Thinking preferences (represented as a left–right bias for these upper and lower hemispheres) are identified using an assessment tool called the Herrmann brain dominance instrument (HBDI).

While our 'whole-brain' behaviour management (WBBM) model encourages adaptation and change (as opposed to relying upon comfortable but possibly ineffective ways of managing behaviour and relating to others) there is certainly no intention to label, categorise or identify teachers according to their preferred ways of thinking, feeling and acting in the classroom. Neither does the model assign specialised modes of thinking into halves or quadrants of the brain. Our model posits that we can *choose* which thoughts we attend to and harness our mental capabilities to effectively rewire our brains and have more control over our relationships and experiences in the classroom. This may sound rather 'hyped up' and idealistic but evidence

| Cerebral left – logical thinking | Cerebral right – visionary thinking |
|---|---|
| Analytical, technical, rational, problem solving | Imaginative, speculative, holistic, creative |
| **Theorists** | **Innovators** |
| **Limbic left – organised thinking** | **Limbic right – communicative thinking** |
| Reliable, orderly, controlled, systematic | Sensitive, empathic, expressive, spiritual |
| **Organisers** | **Humanitarians** |

*Figure 2.1* Herrmann's model.

to support this theory of human potential is gaining pace across a number of disciplines (see Chapter 3), including the field of neuroscience, which is moving faster than ever before owing to technological advances. In this chapter, we provide a brief overview of some of the developments that add weight to this assumption and also highlight some of the neuromyths that have taken hold in the wake of these neuroscientific advances.

## Theories of brain organisation

### The triune brain

In 1973, Paul MacLean, a senior research scientist at the National Institute of Mental Health, proposed that the brain is made up of three distinct subdivisions, each superimposed over the other and corresponding to three consecutive evolutionary eras.

MacLean's theory is known as the triune brain theory.

---

### MacLean's triune brain model

- The reptilian brain – the oldest part of the brain, which is also known as the 'primitive' or archipallium brain. This was the first highly complex neural bundle to appear in evolutionary history and contains the brain stem and the cerebellum. This part of the brain is filled with ancestral memories and works at an unconscious level for survival. It controls semi-automatic reflexes and supports the basic physiological functions such as circulation, respiration, digestion and elimination. It is also involved in mating and territorial behaviour.

- The palaeomammalian brain – also known as the middle brain or limbic system. This is the emotional centre of the brain and also works at an unconscious level. It governs long-term memory, sleeping and eating cycles and higher-order emotions. According to MacLean, as evolution progressed and the protection of offspring became an effective survival strategy, the limbic brain developed to fulfil that function. This part of the brain is divided into two halves or limbic hemispheres that are connected by the hippocampal commissure. This part of the brain contains

the amygdala, hippocampus, hypothalamus, thalamus and pineal gland.
- The neomammalian brain – the neocortex or 'upper' brain is also referred to as the 'rational brain' and was the last part of the brain to evolve. This is also divided into two halves – the left and right cerebral hemispheres – and these are connected by the corpus callosum. The neocortex is the largest and it distinguishes humans from other mammals because it enables us to reason, think, plan, make decisions and be creative. The neocortex comprises the frontal, occipital, parietal and temporal lobes.

When MacLean introduced this theory of the brain it had a significant impact because prior to this it was assumed that the highest level of the brain, the neocortex, dominated the two lower levels. MacLean suggested that the need for survival dominates and when we are threatened (emotionally, physically or psychologically) the brain effectively downshifts and the reptilian brain takes over and hijacks the rational brain.

This paradigm has recently been questioned however by neuroscientists who argue that the linear theory of brain evolution does not sufficiently explain the complexity of the brain's interconnected circuitry. For example, neuroscience now suggests that, although emotional impulse may originate in the limbic system, emotions are regulated by structures that are newer in evolution – within the prefrontal cortex. Damasio (1999) argues that emotions are indispensable for rational thought.

### Hemispheres of the brain

It has long been known that the brain is divided into two linked cerebral hemispheres (left and right) each of which has four distinct lobes (see Figures 2.2 and 2.3):

- frontal – associated with planning and action;
- temporal – associated with hearing, memory and object recognition;
- parietal – associated with sensation and spatial processing;
- occipital – associated with vision.

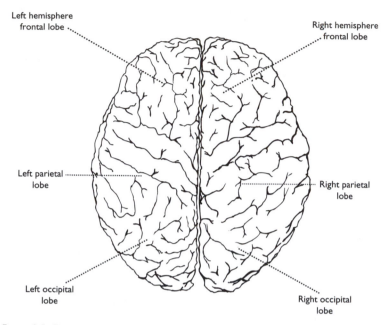

Left hemisphere
frontal lobe

Right hemisphere
frontal lobe

Left parietal
lobe

Right parietal
lobe

Left occipital
lobe

Right occipital
lobe

*Figure 2.2* Dorsal view of the brain.

The two halves or hemispheres of the neocortex are connected by the corpus callosum, which is a large bundle of nerve fibres that joins and transmits messages from one side of the brain to the other. Left and right asymmetry is common in the human body (for example most people have a dominant hand and eye), but over-simplified descriptions of hemispheric specialisation in popular literature and the media have given rise to folk theory about independent functions and hemispheric thinking styles (and even personality styles) that are misleading. The localisation of language in the left hemisphere for example has come to be equated with a rational, analytical and logical thinking style whereas the right hemisphere is equated with a holistic, intuitive and emotional way of thinking.

In recent years, scientists have come to the conclusion that the distinction between the two cerebral hemispheres is a much subtler one that relates to processing style. According to Bruer (1997), the misinterpretation of these scientific findings (regarding functional asymmetries for the processing of stimuli) to create conceptions about hemispheric differences on a different level (such as a cognitive

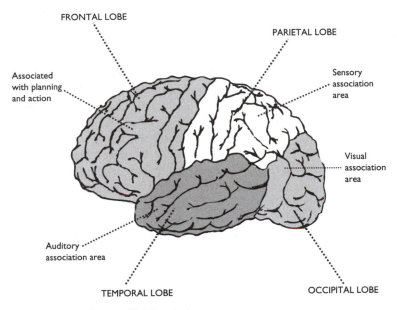

FRONTAL LOBE

PARIETAL LOBE

Associated
with planning
and action

Sensory
association
area

Visual
association
area

Auditory
association area

TEMPORAL LOBE

OCCIPITAL LOBE

*Figure 2.3* Lateral view of left hemisphere.

thinking style) is a 'bridge too far'. There is simply no direct scientific evidence to support the claim. Furthermore, neuroimaging data that show laterality in verbal (left) and non-verbal (right) processing is almost always elicited from right-handed male subjects, whereas language processing in left-handed females is much more likely to be located in the right hemisphere.

The precept that emotions are processed solely in the right hemisphere was challenged by a team of Belgian psychologists (Vingerhoets *et al.*, 2003) who used ultrasound technology to discover what happens when the brain is faced with emotional language as conveyed through voice tone. Participants were attached to ultrasound monitors and listened to pre-recorded sentences. In some cases, sentences were conveyed with emotion; in others they were spoken with a neutral tone. At various times, participants were asked to focus either on the actual words of the sentences or on the emotion conveyed by the speaker's tone and then point to the appropriate emotion on a card. The researchers found that when participants were asked to focus on the semantics (language) the left side of the brain, as expected, showed increased activity. When focusing on the tone of voice used, activity increased on the right side but showed no signs of decreasing in the left hemisphere. This evidence confirmed that the right hemisphere is not exclusively responsible for processing the expression of emotions, and the left brain stays active, probably to categorise or label the emotion.

Theories of brain laterality have also been challenged by cases from medical science where it has been proven that an entire hemisphere of a young epileptic child's brain can be surgically removed without this affecting most normal functions. The 'whole brain' is therefore greater than the sum of its parts and can even continue to function when parts are missing. Even the language function (generally associated with the left hemisphere of a right-handed person) is apparently reassigned to the right cerebral hemisphere and enables the child to talk and read. This phenomenon, known as cross-modal reassignment, also explains why individuals without sight develop acute hearing or sense of touch. This ability of the brain to remap its topography is what is meant by neuroplasticity.

### Brain functions

Within the brain, certain structures are identified with particular functions. For example, the hippocampus appears to be associated with the formation of memories, and the amygdala (the brain's early warning system) with emotional responses; the hypothalamus is thought to regulate homeostasis and the thalamus receives and codes information from the senses (see Figure 2.4).

However, it is increasingly recognised that these specialised functions are 'gross characterisations' and any complex skill actually involves a co-ordinated response from several specialised neural networks in different parts of the brain (OECD, 2002). This 'globalist' view asserts that every mental faculty is shared across the brain, and both hemispheres work in parallel, contributing in a complementary, not exclusive, fashion (McCrone, 1999).

### Neuronal activity

The neocortex contains literally billions of nerve cells or neurons that communicate with one another via chemicals (such as noradrenaline, dopamine, serotonin and endorphins) which are known as neurotransmitters. Potentially, each neuron can connect with thousands of adjoining neurons by transmitting and receiving information in the form of electrochemical messages. These messages are taken in

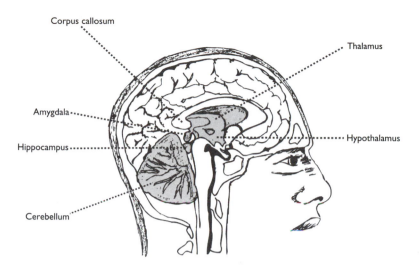

*Figure 2.4* Structures in the brain associated with specialised functions.

through dendrites, which are like tiny receptive branches or antennae at one end of the neuron, and then passed on via the axon at the other end. The synapse is the junction or gap between the dendrites of different neurons (see Figure 2.5) or between the dendrite of one neuron and the axon of another. Neurotransmitters are fired across the synaptic cleft to make the neural connection from one neuron to another, a process known as synaptic sparking. In very simple terms, this process makes up the circuitry of the brain.

It is believed that the neocortex has almost its full complement of nerve cells or neurons from the time of birth but the number of dendrites and the synaptic connections between them undergoes significant change throughout life. During childhood, the dendrites grow (a process also referred to as synaptic sprouting) but then are subsequently 'pruned'. It is thought that 20 billion synapses are pruned every day between childhood and early adolescence (Schwartz and Begley, 2002). Increased levels of synaptic sprouting and pruning occur during infancy, and a considerable body of neurobiological evidence supports the importance of an enriched and stimulating environment in the first few months of life (Whitebread, 2002). A second phase of sprouting and pruning occurs in the frontal lobes just before puberty, which affects emotional regulation, judgement and self-control.

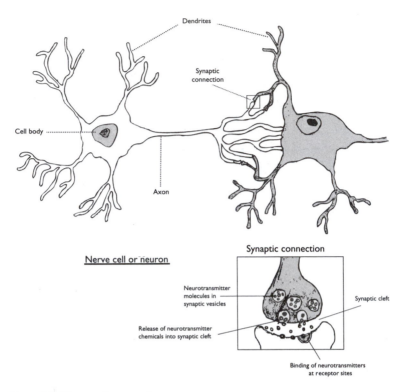

Dendrites

Synaptic connection

Cell body

Axon

Nerve cell or neuron

Synaptic connection

Neurotransmitter molecules in synaptic vesicles

Synaptic cleft

Release of neurotransmitter chemicals into synaptic cleft

Binding of neurotransmitters at receptor sites

*Figure 2.5* Neuronal connection.

Connections between neurons that are activated most frequently are preserved, and once connections are established they become hard-wired pathways that activate spontaneously in new situations. Neurons have to have a good reason to survive and so those connections that are ineffective or weak (rarely activated) are the ones that get pruned. This is the origin of the phrase 'Use it or lose it.' The brain can be likened to an oscillator with electrical activity ebbing and flowing. As we repeatedly stimulate the same chain of networks (or neural pathways) it increases our chances of committing something to memory (practice makes perfect). It has also been found that the synaptic connections in the emotional centre of the brain are more durable or hard-wired than the connections between synapses in other areas (Robertson, 1999).

### Neuroplasticity

> The plasticity of the living matter of our nervous system, in short, is the reason why we do a thing with difficulty the first time, but soon do it more and more easily, and finally, with sufficient practice, do it semi-mechanically, or with hardly any consciousness at all. Our nervous systems have grown to the way in which they have been exercised, just as a sheet of paper or a coat, once creased or folded, tends to fall forever afterward into the same identical folds.
>
> (James, 2005 [1899]: 32)

At the end of the nineteenth century, William James dared to suggest that habitual behaviours were expressions of plastic changes in the physical substrate of our minds. This flew in the face of conventional wisdom at that time; scientists asserted that plasticity was something that only applied to the brain of the young child. It has only been in the last twenty years or so that neuroscientists have discovered that the adult brain is not structurally immutable after all. Neuroplasticity is the capacity of neurons to forge new connections and literally 'rewire' the brain. Repeated experiences actually help shape and alter the morphology of the brain itself, and this neural plasticity is now known to continue throughout life. According to Schwartz and Begley (2002: 366), this process is more likely to occur when the individual pays 'mindful attention' to the experience or stimulation. What's more, Schwartz and Begley also propose that mental force alone can be used to self-direct neuroplasticity. (See Chapter 3 for research evidence to support this claim.) In his description of his work with the physicist Henry Stapp, Schwartz establishes the basic mechanics of self-directed neuroplasticity in quantum physics, and reveals its connections with the ancient practice of mindfulness in Buddhist traditions.

### Mirror neurons

Another major neuroscientific breakthrough of recent times is the discovery about the roots of empathy. Giaccamo Rizzollatti's discovery of 'mirror neurons' in the frontal lobes of monkeys found that certain brain cells fired when a monkey performed a single, highly specific action with its hand such as picking up and putting a peanut in its mouth. The research team discovered that not only did different neurons fire in response to different actions but any given mirror neuron also fired when the monkeys observed another monkey, or even a scientist, perform the same action (Rizzollatti and Craighero, 2004).

Building on from this research, there is now evidence (from fMRI[1] neuroimaging technology) that complex multiple mirror systems exist in humans (Austin, 2006). These specialise in carrying out and understanding not only the actions of others but also their emotions and even their intentions. Mirror neurons are capable therefore of providing us with the basis for extending our understanding of the human mind, including empathy and imitation learning. This even extends to 'mind reading', for example predicting what someone will do with an object that he/she has picked up. Such evidence confirms that we are 'wired' to connect with one another. When we watch another person do something, the corresponding mirror neuron fires in our brain, enabling us to read and understand the other person's intentions. Coaching methods such as visualisation and imagery have been using these neuronal mirror properties for a number of years without us really understanding their biological basis.

'Whole-brain' behaviour management has been influenced by all these important neuroscientific developments and is underpinned by the following principles:

- Most brain functions occur bilaterally (in both hemispheres).
- The whole brain is greater than the sum of its parts.
- Emotions are indispensable for rational thought.
- The brain is malleable throughout life.
- We can choose the thoughts we attend to.
- Mindful attention enables us to shape our brains.
- Humans are hard-wired to connect with one another.

The following chapter illustrates further connections between neuroscientific findings, other key disciplinary influences and the development of the 'whole-brain' model of behaviour management.

# Chapter 3

# Sorting and grouping

Science without religion is lame; religion without science is blind.

All religions, arts and sciences are branches of the same tree.
(Albert Einstein, 1879–1955)

Einstein claimed that the concepts of science (methodical thinking that leads us to knowledge) and religion (emotional and ethical aspects of human thinking as opposed to organised religion or mono-theism) are connected in a strong, reciprocal relationship and that emotions are the driving force behind all human achievement.

This chapter will provide further insight for those who are inter-ested in understanding more about this reciprocal relationship and other connections between the key theoretical influences that helped to inform and shape the WBBM model. The chief spheres of influ-ence can be identified as philosophy of mind, cognitive and affec-tive neuroscience, spirituality, and social and positive psychology. These will be explored in turn, although we recognise that it is somewhat artificial to separate the different sources we have drawn upon.

## Philosophy of mind

The ancient concept of dualism, which can be traced back to early Greek philosophers such as Plato, asserts the separate existence of mind and body (including the brain) and is generally attributed to the work of René Descartes (1596–1650). Descartes divided nature into a physical realm and a mental realm and described the body as an automaton (a kind of moving machine) motivated by physical laws, which performs functions that are independent of the soul. Antonio Damasio (1994), a Portuguese neuroscientist, humanist and philosopher, challenges this paradigm in his book *Descartes' Error* and provides evidence of the central role of emotions in decision making and rational thought. He argues that rationality is built on emotion and cannot exist without it. Damasio also makes a distinction between emotion (which comes first and is public and visible to others) and feeling (which follows emotion and is internal and private to the individual).

The mind–brain enigma is an age-old philosophical debate; are the mind and brain one and the same thing? Conventional science long held the position that the mind is an illusion, a side effect of electrochemical activity in the physical brain, but (as suggested in Chapter 2) recent developments in neuroscience have demonstrated that the human mind is an independent entity that can shape and change the physical structure and circuitry of the brain (Schwartz and Begley, 2002).

## Cognitive and affective neuroscience

As discussed in the previous chapter, it used to be assumed that the brain of a child was malleable and plastic but the structure and functional organisation of the adult human brain was immutable (hard-wired in a way to prevent further development). This conventional wisdom of the day became a tenet of neuroscience and remained unchallenged for the first half of the twentieth century.

The discipline of neuroscience has its roots in medical pathology, which generated a considerable amount of research data in support of localised or specialist brain functions. This data derived mainly from invasive studies (involving surgery) of patients with a brain injury or lesions in certain parts of their brain that resulted in the loss of a particular function. Some lesion studies concluded that specific cognitive functions are localised in certain areas or structures of the brain. Other studies have demonstrated that other parts of the brain literally 'take over' and compensate for injury without apparent deficit. Proponents of the former view are known as 'localists' and of the latter as 'globalists'. Recent schools of thought seem to accept that, although some parts of the brain do appear to have specialist functions, the brain works in a much more integrated way than was previously believed. It is also becoming clear that environmental differences can play an important role in the way that the brain functions. For example, in the brains of individuals who are born deaf, the area of the brain normally associated with auditory analysis is used for spatial analysis (Goswami, 2004).

In recent years, developments in cognitive neuroscience have accelerated as a result of the continual refinement of technology used to investigate neuronal activity and measure changes in the brain. Notably, the use of PET (positron emission tomography) scans and fMRI (functional magnetic resonance imaging) enables neuroscientists to observe the brain in action and make connections between human behaviour and levels of metabolic activity.

In 1997, Gage discovered that, when adult mice were placed in an enriched environment, new brain cells grew in part of the hippocampus. In 1998, Gage (and others) went on to make a major scientific breakthrough when they discovered that new cells could also grow in the dentate gyrus region of the human adult hippocampus, an area of the brain associated with learning, memory and emotion (Eriksson *et al.*, 1998). This process is known as neurogenesis, literally meaning the birth of neurons, and involves the transformation of stem cells. Neuroplasticity or brain malleability is the ability to form new neural connections through training and experience. This capacity to 'rewire' the brain enables us to cope with the ever-changing challenges that we are presented with throughout our entire life. Over the last fifteen years or so there has been an explosion of studies on neuroplasticity, with modern neuroscience now demonstrating and confirming what William James dared to suggest more than a century ago, before his ideas were quashed by the rise of behaviourism, deterministic physics and logical positivism (Maslow, 1968: 14).

Maguire *et al.* (2000; cited in Schwartz and Begley, 2002) conducted a study involving sixteen London cab drivers and found that, compared to the brain scans of fifty non-cab drivers, their scans showed that the rear portion of the hippocampus (which is responsible for directional memories) was enlarged. In order to test the hypothesis that they had not simply gravitated towards a career in which this cognitive ability was required, the researchers introduced the variable of experience and found a positive correlation between the size of the posterior hippocampus and the length of time the subjects had worked as cab drivers. These findings demonstrated that the taxi drivers' brains changed in structure as a result of them 'paying attention' to spatial and directional mental functions.

Schwartz and Begley (2002) have produced a range of evidence to suggest that the power of the mind, or applied mindfulness, can change neuronal circuitry. They refer to this as 'self-directed brain changes' (p. 94). In their studies of people with obsessive-compulsive disorder (OCD) they found that, with training, people could use conscious thought to relabel and dismiss the invading obsessive thoughts and compulsive urges and, furthermore, this process could lead to observable changes to neural pathways in the brain. Schwartz and Begley also refer to an experiment conducted by Pascual-Leone in 1995 which proved that even mental rehearsal and visual imagery (of piano playing) could strengthen synapses and produce observable changes in the brain. They also describe other studies conducted with stroke patients and those suffering from clinical depression and concluded that applied mindfulness (thinking about one's own emotions and thoughts from an impartial spectator position) could help people to alter their brain circuitry (ibid.). These findings provide empirical evidence to support the hypothesis that directed mental force can lead to self-directed neuroplasticity.

Schwartz's concept of mental force is also related to ancient Buddhist concepts of mindfulness and karma. He concludes that the conscious and wilful mind is distinct from the brain and cannot be explained solely by the matter or material substance of the brain. The simple act of paying attention can produce physical changes in the brain. Research involving Tibetan Buddhist monks and the activity of meditation (Davidson *et al.*, 2003) revealed a link between compassionate meditation and actual structural synaptic and neural changes in the brain, which were observable through scans. These results were presented at the annual meeting of the Society for Neuroscience in Washington, DC, in November 2005, which was opened by the Dalai Lama. The Dalai Lama attests that Buddhism and science share the common objective of serving humanity and developing a better understanding of the world. He maintains in his teachings that science can offer powerful tools for understanding the interconnectedness of all life and encourages Buddhist practitioners to blend their spiritual knowledge with modern scientific knowledge.

Despite the mass of data on brain functioning that neuroscientific research is revealing, it could be argued that scientists are raising more questions than they are answering. According to Panksepp (1998) one of the most important and most neglected topics in neuroscience is the attempt to understand exactly how emotional feelings are generated. He refers to this as affective neuroscience. The main problem is that it is not ethical to study the human brain in sufficient depth to understand how emotional systems actually operate.

Damasio (1999, 2003) appears to have built on Panksepp's earlier work, developing a neuroscientific theory of emotion and feeling which is founded on human and animal survival and the need for homeostasis. Damasio postulates that all feelings and emotions are rooted in the organism's need to retain optimum balance of bodily states. He also maintains that the brain structures responsible for reasoning and emotions cooperate and partly overlap and communicate with the rest of the body. Psychoneuroimmunology is a relatively new field of study which explores the connections between the nervous system, the immune system and states of mind. There is a growing body of evidence to suggest that the quality of our relationships can actually affect our health (Goleman, 2006) and that the body is capable of producing the chemicals it requires to heal itself (Chopra, 1989).

Subjective experience is the essential reality in quantum theory and, over the past century, quantum physicists have begun to untangle some of the mysteries of the universe and gather data that challenges us to revise our view of reality and to acknowledge that we simply do not know what exists in the quantum domain. This takes us beyond the realm of what we currently 'know' to be 'real'.

## Spirituality

Science and spirituality have historically trodden entirely separate paths. One is rational and objective whereas the other is subjective and intuitive. The materialist paradigm, which has dominated Western science, upholds the dogma that only the physical is ontologically valid, denying the reality of subjective states of sentience. In other words, anything that is immaterial is mystical, non-scientific and therefore invalid. However, as Einstein observed (see the opening quote of the chapter), this may be an artificial discord, as both disciplines aim to understand the world and may therefore be seen as mutually compatible. In recent years there has been a discernible convergence between these sources of wisdom (for example in the field of medicine and meditation) that reflects a shift towards a more interdisciplinary and holistic approach.

Spirituality is considered here in its widest sense. It is not confined to religion or theology but can refer to any source of inspiration, awe or wonder that impacts on an individual's identity or sense of purpose. Matthews (2006) describes spirituality as the way in which individuals respond reflectively in thought, physically and in feelings to events and experiences (p. 17). Spiritual growth is about personal transformation and the belief that life is a process of moving towards enhanced awareness. It is within this context that links become apparent between spirituality and the WBBM model.

Spiritual influences that are not linked specifically to a major faith include Mike George (2003), who explores the inner soul and promotes the power of self-knowledge, and Marilyn Ferguson (1980), who also attempts to bring various disciplinary strands together to explain the next stage of evolution for human beings. James Redfield shares this vision of human evolution and reveals the stages (or insights) through a series of parables (Redfield and Adrienne, 1995). Part of his theory, which has influenced our model, is that of energy exchange and the principle that positive energy fuels and motivates individuals to self-actualise.

It can be hard to separate these kinds of texts that focus on transformation through personal growth (see also Louise Hay, 1984, and Susan Jeffers, 1988) from more orthodox spiritual teachings. This is because essentially both are founded on the belief that we can move away from our limiting views of ourselves by transforming our thoughts, beliefs and actions. Those who perceive it to be superficial psychobabble often ridicule the explosion in self-development literature, but we would argue that the basic principles are sound and grounded in a range of Eastern and ancient spiritual teachings that have stood the test of time.

Buddhist tradition places a great deal of emphasis on self-awareness, psychological well-being, emotional intelligence, compassion and mindfulness. For example, the Tibetan term *Lo-jong* means training or transforming the mind and implies inner discipline (or emotional regulation). This links with the core principles of WBBM in that, by training ourselves to develop new perspectives, we can change our thinking and our behaviour. In recent years, there has been increasing dialogue between Western scientists and the Dalai Lama about the relationship between mind, body and spirit (Goleman, 1997). Yoga is concerned with synchronising mind, body and spirit through meditation. Indian yogic traditions posit the existence of three energy channels (*nadis*) associated with reasoning, emotion and spiritual evolution. The purpose of yoga techniques is to achieve mastery over the mind, body and emotional self (emotional intelligence).

From Christianity, the work of Norman Vincent Peale (1996 [1953]), whose influential book *The Power of Positive Thinking* remains in print today, proffers that belief can be a great support and an antidote to feelings of inadequacy and insecurity. 'Feelings of confidence depend on the type of thoughts that habitually occupy your mind. Think defeat and you are bound to be defeated . . . Formulate and stamp indelibly on your mind a mental picture of yourself as succeeding' (pp. 16–17).

Emotional regulation is also integral to the seventh and eight principles of Kabbalah, the ancient teachings of Abraham (*circa* 2000 BC) which lay the foundations for the world's major religions. These principles make reference to 'resistance', which enables us to recognise and manage our emotional responses in a way that avoids damaging relationships and enables us to grow as individuals. 'Consistent effort at resistance will progressively cleanse reckless behaviour, selfish desires and negative thoughts from your nature' (Berg, 2003: 137).

## Social psychology

Social psychology is concerned with the nature and causes of human social behaviour. It seeks to understand and explain how human individuals relate, communicate, exert influence over one another and affect one another's behaviour. The links between social psychology and behaviour management in the classroom could not be more obvious, and four of the six domains that make up the WBBM wheel of competencies (see Chapter 5) are strongly associated with this discipline (communication, self-efficacy, emotional literacy and psychology).

The way that we perceive and interpret behaviour can be explained by theories of attribution proposed by psychologists such as Fritz Heider and Harold Kelley. Heider (1958) believed that individuals (including teachers) act on the basis of their beliefs, and Kelley (1967) explained how our attributions are influenced by a combination of personal experience and other people's perceptions (consensus). The development of the WBBM model was also heavily influenced by the work of the social psychologist Albert Bandura, who developed the concept of self-efficacy (one of the six domains of our model).

Another psychological theory that resonates closely with the key tools and aims of the WBBM model is that of transactional analysis

(TA). The key principles behind the theory and philosophy of TA are that people are OK and everyone has the capacity to change, grow, think and make decisions about their destiny. One of the key concepts of TA is that of 'strokes'. Strokes are units of human recognition and these can be verbal or non-verbal, conditional or unconditional, and positive or negative, but because human individuals are 'wired' for connecting with one another (Goleman, 2006) we need, and seek to receive, whatever strokes we can. This means that humans sometimes 'invite' negative strokes rather than have none at all. Eric Berne (the father of TA) (1961) also described how our behaviour is driven and shaped by unconscious messages that we received in early childhood. The five 'drivers' described by Berne as 'Be perfect', 'Please others', 'Be strong', 'Try hard' and 'Hurry up' are manifested as consistent behavioural patterns. A growing number of teachers are beginning to use aspects of transactional analysis to help them understand their own and their students' behaviour and to improve the quality of relationships in the classroom (Barrow and Newton, 2004). Read more about the ego state model and patterns of transaction in Chapter 9 (on communication).

Similarly, neurolinguistic programming (NLP) offers another vehicle for understanding and making connections between the ways that people think, behave, learn and change and is an approach that is becoming incorporated into the classroom by some teachers. In the WBBM model, the recognition that we may have preferred modalities or ways of making sense of the world chimes with the principles of NLP. In both these approaches there is the premise that we are 'programmed' by our past experiences but with mindful attention we can change states; our personal perceptions and beliefs can be challenged, and changes in cognition and behaviour can be introduced.

## Positive psychology

Positive psychology focuses primarily on the empirical study of human flourishing and valued subjective experience. This is a relatively new branch of psychology that has only been in vogue for about ten years or so but its roots go back much further than that. For example, when Maslow criticised the reductionistic and mechanistic views of psychology promoted by the behaviourists and psychoanalysts, he called for a psychological science, which could study optimal psychological health, including the human spirit (Maslow,

1968). Other early representations of what we would now consider as positive psychology can be found in studies of marital happiness (Terman, 1938), effective parenting (Watson, 1928) and the meaning of life (Jung, 1933).

Martin Seligman is regarded as the founder and key proponent in the field of positive psychology. He argues that because human beings evolved during times of environmental stress (famine, ice, flood, etc.) we developed 'catastrophic' brains that are literally programmed to look for things that are wrong and react to perceived threat. Western psychology is founded on a tradition of focusing mainly on a 'disease' model of investigating human behaviour and has been dominated by studies of 'abnormal' behaviour such as neurosis, schizophrenia, anxiety, etc. Seligman argues that psychology should not be limited to the study of pathology, weakness and damage but should embrace the study of personal strength and qualities such as virtue, courage and altruism.

According to Seligman, individuals interpret events in different ways owing to their habitual 'explanatory style' (they choose how to explain setbacks to themselves), and this is linked to their levels of optimism or pessimism. He developed a construct known as 'learned optimism' (Seligman, 1998), which is about defeating self-limiting inner thought patterns and regulating one's own emotions. Within the WBBM model, this relates closely to the core tool of resolute optimism (p. 49) and the domains of emotional literacy and self-efficacy (Chapters 10 and 11).

Positive psychology is multi-dimensional in that it can be applied to individuals and groups as well as over time. For example, it might explore valued subjective experiences such as satisfaction (about events in the past), hope and optimism (for the future), and flow and happiness (in the present state). At the individual level it focuses on positive personal traits such as the capacity for love, courage, interpersonal connection, perseverance and forgiveness. At the group level it is about civic virtues and social ethics that move individuals toward better citizenship, group responsibility, tolerance and a positive work ethic (Seligman and Czikszentmihalyi, 2000).

This chapter has provided some insight into the range of interdisciplinary influences that have helped to shape and underpin the 'whole-brain' behaviour model. Although this represents a seemingly diverse set of ideas and developments, they are linked in many ways, all of which underline the capacity for human growth.

# Chapter 4

# Identifying the boundaries

It is not enough to understand what we ought to be, unless we know what we are.

(T.S. Eliot, 1888–1965)

In Chapter 1, it was suggested that the concept of metacognition ('thinking about thinking') could be applied to professional development and behaviour management. If we accept that metacognition enables individuals to develop a conscious awareness of their modes of thought through a reflective process of higher-order thinking and attending to mental activity (for example self-questioning, making connections, taking appropriate action, self-monitoring and regulating thoughts) then the same metacognitive strategies can enable us to 'think about how we think' in our roles as managers of behaviour in the classroom. This is a central tenet of the WBBM model.

A metacognitive approach encourages teachers to enhance self-knowledge by:

- identifying what it is they know and don't yet know about their own thoughts, feelings and actions;
- talking about their thoughts, feelings and actions, which may be achieved by establishing a peer coaching model (see Chapter 5) or through less formal approaches;
- making decisions about the changes that are required or wanted;
- keeping a journal or diary to help them reflect on the development of their thinking;

> • assuming personal responsibility by self-regulating and self-monitoring (rather than relying on another person to set the targets for them).

The first step is often the most difficult one because it requires a determination on the part of the individual to 'get to the truth' no matter how uncomfortable that process might be. When things are regularly going less than well in the classroom, it is easy for any teacher to become despondent, demotivated and lacking in sufficient energy to find effective solutions (see Chapter 11 on self-efficacy). Such teachers are (according to their own perception) 'consciously ineffective' (Rogers, 1992). They know that they need to improve certain aspects of their practice but feel overwhelmed, inadequate or disempowered and are therefore unable to make the necessary changes.

Some teachers, on the other hand, may choose not to recognise their own contribution to the difficult situation in which they find themselves and apportion the blame to someone else, usually the student(s), or they may convince themselves that things are going well when clearly there are problems (as perceived by the students, colleagues, parents, etc.). This mind-set is sometimes referred to as 'unconscious ineffectiveness'.

The first objective of the metacognitive approach to behaviour management is to attain the third level of development or what Rogers calls 'connective awareness'. In other words, teachers are aware of what it is they need or want to work on (knowing that they know). Once this level is achieved, teachers can become 'consciously effective' (I know what to do, think and say and I am starting to put it into practice) and, ultimately (when the synaptic connections become established), unconsciously effective (and just do it without thinking).

In this chapter we introduce a simple self-reporting instrument that may help teachers to begin this process of reflecting on their cognitions (thoughts), affects (feelings) and behaviour (actions).

## Introduction to the CAB profile

The CAB profile is a simple inventory that consists of a list of fifty-four present-tense dispositional statements which teachers consider in turn and then make a decision as to whether or not the statement 'sounds like them'.

It is important to state at the outset that this tool has not been psychometrically evaluated or standardised in any way. It has however been trialled informally and developed with a cohort of 100 trainee teachers as part of a professional studies course, a group of primary school teachers as part of a programme of whole-school professional development and also as part of a research project in which pairs of teachers used the WBBM model as the basis for peer coaching. In all cases, participants used the instrument to provide a focus for shared or private reflection on their practice.

Neither is the instrument designed to assign or categorise teachers into 'types'. The purpose of the inventory is to help teachers begin to think about their 'preferred' cognitive, affective and behavioural responses in particular circumstances and to identify their personal profile across the six competency domains. This, in turn, may enable teachers to recognise, prioritise and focus on specific areas of professional development.

Self-reporting instruments like the CAB profile are notoriously flawed in terms of their susceptibility to respondent bias. Even though results are private to the individual, there may still be a conditioned tendency to opt for socially or professionally 'acceptable' responses. The use of the instrument is entirely optional, and this approach will not appeal to all readers. We also recognise that the measure of self-awareness is probably more effectively judged in action and through reflection of *actual* circumstances rather than considering a set of generalised judgements, which is why each chapter contains opportunities for readers to enhance self-knowledge by relating what they read about other 'teachers' to their own practice and experiences in the classroom.

### Instructions for using the CAB profiling tool

- Take your time to consider each statement and reflect carefully before making a decision.
- To get the most from the exercise try to make your responses as true for you as you can. Remember, there are no right or wrong answers.
- Having made the decision that this either sounds like you or doesn't sound like you, place a tick in the relevant column alongside each statement.
- If you really can't decide then tick the 'unsure' box.

- When all statements have been considered, turn to the key and profile sheet in the Appendix.
- Use the key provided to shade in the profile sheet (Figure A.1). For each tick you have placed in the 'This sounds like me' column, shade in one section of the relevant profile bar.
- The completed profile will provide a visual representation of your relative strengths in each domain of the WBBM wheel of competencies (see Chapter 5).

Tick the most appropriate column for each item in Table 4.1.

*Table 4.1* CAB profiling tool

|  |  | This sounds like me | Not sure | This doesn't sound like me |
|---|---|---|---|---|
| 1 | I'm the kind of person who will ask lots of questions if I don't know something. |  |  |  |
| 2 | I seem to know instinctively how others are feeling. |  |  |  |
| 3 | I usually arrive in good time for lessons, appointments and meetings. |  |  |  |
| 4 | I tend to get elected as a spokesperson. |  |  |  |
| 5 | I usually look on the bright side of life. |  |  |  |
| 6 | I handle myself well during arguments and can usually reach a compromise. |  |  |  |

*Continued Overleaf*

*Table 4.1* Continued

| | | This sounds like me | Not sure | This doesn't sound like me |
|---|---|---|---|---|
| 7 | I will often seek advice from other people or books in order to make a better job of things even if this means delaying a task. | | | |
| 8 | I'm the sort of person who likes to know exactly what to expect when faced with new or unfamiliar situations. | | | |
| 9 | I am good at finding my own solutions to any worries or problems that I face. | | | |
| 10 | People often confide in me or tell me that I'm a good listener. | | | |
| 11 | I always make a point of learning from my mistakes rather than feeling defeated or knocked back by them. | | | |
| 12 | I think people would describe me as very courteous and polite. | | | |
| 13 | Time management is one of my strengths. | | | |
| 14 | I try to make sense of and analyse my own behaviour. | | | |
| 15 | I normally bounce back quickly after a disappointment. | | | |

| 16 | Structure and routines are important to me. | | | |
|----|---|---|---|---|
| 17 | I get a real buzz from sharing new ideas and things I have learned. | | | |
| 18 | I believe that people make their own luck in this world. | | | |
| 19 | I'm the sort of person who likes to plan things well ahead. | | | |
| 20 | I'm interested in psychological theory. | | | |
| 21 | I'm a mediator and good at resolving arguments between other people. | | | |
| 22 | I like to read up about places before I visit them. | | | |
| 23 | I understand the difference between behaviourist and cognitive approaches to behaviour management. | | | |
| 24 | I almost always keep calm in difficult situations. | | | |
| 25 | I am efficient at managing paperwork and record keeping. | | | |
| 26 | I am not easily intimidated by people or challenging situations. | | | |
| 27 | I always try to consider the other person's point of view whenever there is a conflict of views, wants or needs. | | | |

*Continued Overleaf*

*Table 4.1* Continued

|  |  | This sounds like me | Not sure | This doesn't sound like me |
|---|---|---|---|---|
| 28 | I always try to read and keep up with current ideas in education. |  |  |  |
| 29 | I am good at calming people down or cheering them up. |  |  |  |
| 30 | I can't bear mess. |  |  |  |
| 31 | I am fascinated by human relationships and I enjoy films and novels that explore this dimension. |  |  |  |
| 32 | I know I have the potential to succeed in the things I want to achieve. |  |  |  |
| 33 | I can accept compliments and positive feedback without embarrassment or dismissal. |  |  |  |
| 34 | I get enormous satisfaction from passing on knowledge to others. |  |  |  |
| 35 | It is important for me to understand the underlying reasons for a particular or 'challenging' behaviour. |  |  |  |
| 36 | I hardly ever shout or raise my voice unnecessarily. |  |  |  |
| 37 | I seek out and embrace new ideas and exciting challenges. |  |  |  |

| 38 | I reckon people would describe me as 'good company'. | | | |
|----|----|----|----|----|
| 39 | I am intrigued by what makes people tick. | | | |
| 40 | I go to conferences and lectures whenever possible – to keep up with developments in my field(s) of interest. | | | |
| 41 | I'm known as the one who carries spare tissues/pens/meeting documents/cash, etc. just in case . . . | | | |
| 42 | I rarely sulk or storm off when someone upsets me. | | | |
| 43 | I am known to have an enthusiastic interest in certain subjects (arts/science/history/music, etc.). | | | |
| 44 | I am often conscious of body language (both my own and other people's). | | | |
| 45 | I often find myself puzzling over why someone is behaving in a particular way. | | | |
| 46 | I usually stop and think before I speak my mind. | | | |
| 47 | I know what I'm good at and I build on my strengths. | | | |
| 48 | I can express my needs without being overly apologetic or awkward about it. | | | |

*Continued Overleaf*

*Table 4.1* Continued

| | | This sounds like me | Not sure | This doesn't sound like me |
|---|---|---|---|---|
| 49 | It is important to me to have a place for everything and everything in its place. | | | |
| 50 | I am able to say 'no' to people without losing their respect. | | | |
| 51 | I can think of several approaches and classroom strategies that are influenced by a humanistic perspective on behaviour. | | | |
| 52 | When I get angry, I am unlikely to swear or start crying. | | | |
| 53 | It is a priority of mine to learn new things and try to expand my knowledge. | | | |
| 54 | I continuously monitor and assess the effectiveness of the rewards and sanctions that I use in the classroom. | | | |

# Chapter 5

# Seeing the whole picture

'Whole-brain' behaviour management (WBBM) is a conceptual model that seeks to identify, encapsulate, describe and synthesise a range of diverse elements which, together, constitute effective practice in classroom behaviour management. Unlike other approaches for managing behaviour, which concentrate largely on the development of communication skills, for example, or on organisational aspects of classroom management, this is very much a holistic model that recognises a broader source of influences. An underlying aim of the model is to provide teachers with the means of 'seeing the whole picture' in relation to 'problem' or 'challenging' behaviour in the classroom by helping them to understand the functional relationship and interconnectedness of all these constituent parts.

To lose sight of the whole – this might be the 'whole person' as in all aspects of human functioning, or it might be the whole as in all aspects of the relationship between the teacher and student, or it might be the whole as in the context of the school or local community – is to limit the value of what you are doing. The 'whole' can take many forms and is usually highly complex, but this is not an argument for ignoring its importance. In this chapter, we will describe in detail what the model looks like and explain how it is applied, introduce four key tools for effective behaviour management and suggest a suitable method for using the model in practice (peer coaching).

## What the model looks like

The WBBM model is not just an abstract view; it can be represented visually as a three-dimensional sphere that is composed of six major segments, rather like a peeled orange (see Figure 5.1).

*Figure 5.1* Visual representation of the WBBM model.

Each of the six segments represents a 'domain' or aspect of personal and professional competency related to behaviour management, and each domain is further divided into finer segments ('components') which describe areas of competency within each domain. The reason why our model is perceived as a sphere is that it requires all of its segments in order to be complete or whole. A missing segment would seriously impair the beauty, form and function of the whole – just as, within our model, to be lacking key skills or knowledge in any given domain or even a competency within a domain can impair a teacher's ability to manage behaviour effectively (we need 'every piece of the puzzle'). The central strand, which runs throughout the length of the sphere, represents the set of core principles that are woven into and permeate the entire model. It binds the segments (domains) together and keeps the structure in place. These core principles are respect and value for the individual and living with integrity. Finally, the connective roots that are visible within the sphere represent the dynamic relationship, communication and overlap that exist between the segments (domains and components).

To examine the model more closely, it is necessary to imagine looking down on the orange-like sphere after it has been sliced in half horizontally. Having opened up the model in this way, we see a wheel that is divided initially into the six key domains of personal and professional competency: psychology, knowledge, organisation, communication, emotional literacy and self-efficacy. This is the WBBM wheel of competencies. It is important to note here that each domain is represented by a different colour (although, for the illustrations in this book, we have had to use shades of grey rather than the actual colour). The colour associated with each domain is therefore written in Figure 5.2.

Each of these domains can be opened out and further subdivided into six finer components (see Figure 5.3). In Part II, a separate chapter is devoted to exploring each domain with its six integral and related components in turn. It is necessary to emphasise once more at this point that the model is divided into discrete domains and components for easier presentation in order to help clarify the theory. However, it is important to understand that the divisions are essentially artificial and that there are numerous connections and overlaps between them all. The spherical model allows for the interrelationships between the constituent parts: for example there are obvious links between communication and emotional literacy, and between

*Figure 5.2* The WBBM wheel of competencies.

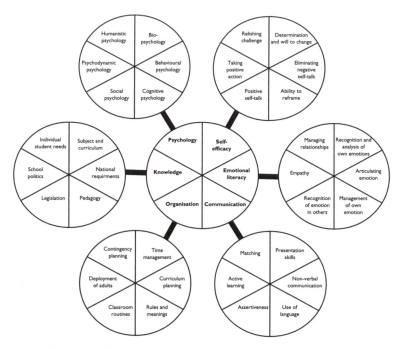

*Figure 5.3* The WBBM model.

knowledge and self-efficacy and so on. Each domain within the model is equally important for behaviour management, and 'whole-brain' thinking assumes that we should try to achieve a 'balanced' wheel by addressing those domains that are generally weaker than others. At a deeper level of analysis, we also need to achieve balance between the components within each domain.

## Four personal tools for effective behaviour management

We suggest that there are four fundamental inner resources or personal tools that underpin successful practice and, like the core principles, these interweave the model. We refer to these throughout the book as the 4 Rs.

---

***Four Rs for effective behaviour management***

- **Responsibility** – the resolve to move from a victim state to one in which personal control is regained.
- **Resilience** – the ability to bounce back from difficult experiences and face challenging situations knowing that you have the inner resource to cope.
- **Receptiveness** – the willingness or readiness to receive new ideas, influences, suggestions or impressions.
- **Resolute optimism** – a belief that you can do something to change any given situation for the better.

---

These personal tools are integral to the model and are therefore referred to frequently (and appear in bold) throughout the second part of this book. Reminding ourselves that we can access these private, inner resources at all times can be very empowering for the teacher. The four Rs are now explored in turn.

The first personal tool within our model is **responsibility**, which we consider in its broadest and deepest sense. This tool requires the teacher to accept responsibility for every aspect of his/her own experience and to accept that energy is depleted only by our perceptual choices rather than by other people's actions or events that take place. It's not what people do and say; it's what we do with what people do and say. By taking responsibility for all that is experienced, the teacher gains the empowerment and energy to make positive changes, promoting personal growth and development. Fundamentally, the personally 'responsible' teacher will be able to accept the impact of his/her own behaviour on that of the students. We are not suggesting here that teachers intentionally (or even unintentionally) invite inappropriate behaviour from their students; neither are we implying that teachers choose to 'imagine' poor behaviour in the classroom. But personally 'responsible' teachers will be able to reflect objectively on their own contribution and response to any interaction or event and this includes their inner feelings as well as how they respond outwardly.

In essence, this is demonstrating internal locus of control as opposed to external locus of control (Rotter, 1966). External locus of control creates a way of thinking that makes the individual a victim of circumstances; things just happen to the individual and all limitations are perceived as being outside of his/her control. The blame for every negative experience is directed at other people and, instead of taking credit for one's own successes and achievements, this is attributed instead to luck, fluke or somebody else's efforts. This mind-set is the opposite of being responsible.

In the context of behaviour management, the personally responsible teacher is one who reflects on his/her practice and considers what changes could be made to pre-empt and resolve behaviour difficulties for individual students. This is the teacher who is prepared to admit his/her mistakes in handling specific situations and who feels comfortable about apologising. Furthermore, such a teacher will take whatever steps are necessary to build bridges to restore relationships with students, parents and colleagues. The responsible teacher has the courage to assertively express his/her needs and feelings directly to a colleague rather than venting frustration and anger to others and not addressing the issue directly. Taking responsibility also means seeking appropriate solutions for oneself rather than habitually referring the problem to a senior colleague.

---

### Ways to improve responsibility

- Remind yourself that you are responsible for your own thoughts and actions.
- Tell yourself that you will handle whatever life throws you.
- Question the concept of a higher authority (school manager, local authority, etc.) having ultimate responsibility for how you conduct yourself in school. The only person who can control you is you!
- See your purpose clearly and see the value and importance of your role as an educator in the life of each and every student you work with.
- Be more aware that everything that you say and do in the classroom has an impact on the lives of your students, shaping their perceptions of themselves and the world.

---

The second personal tool is that of **resilience**. This characteristic includes the ability to restore oneself and bounce back following a difficult experience in order to be able to move on and learn from what happened. Resilience is not giving in to fear and anxiety, which are in themselves immobilising, but having the courage to repeat situations (that were previously problematic) with greater confidence. This confidence comes from the knowledge that you will be able to handle your reactions better next time round. It is about having tenacity and perseverance even though it might be an easier option to give up. Resilient teachers are also better able to maintain a sense of proportion when things do not go according to plan.

In practical terms, the resilient teacher is able to start afresh after a particularly bad day, having philosophically examined what occurred and considered how to limit the possibility of such problems arising again. Although his/her self-belief may be dented, it is not irretrievably undermined when attempts to manage a difficult situation fail. The resilient teacher is also able to accept, for example, that a student acting out in an abusive way towards him/her is not necessarily making a personal assault and is able to see this instead as an indication of the child's emotional needs. Resilience is closely linked to the self-efficacy domain (see Chapter 11).

---

### Ways to improve resilience

- Recognise your importance in the educative process and value yourself highly.
- Be self-aware and recognise your energy needs so that you can maintain yourself.
- Use positive self-talk to affirm your skills and attributes.
- Guard against negative self-talk, which can de-energise you.
- Talk to a trusted individual to help you maintain your self-belief.
- Some people may benefit from spiritual support and others may benefit from counselling to discover their inner strength.

---

To be **receptive** (the third key tool) to new ideas and ways of understanding requires a high level of flexibility of thinking and a willingness to consider alternative perspectives. It presupposes a degree of confidence in one's own perception, opinion and cognition balanced by the acceptance that there are other valid ways of perceiving and thinking (multiple realities). The opposite of receptiveness is to be bound by limited and limiting perspectives, and living with the anxiety that if a certain course of action or way of thinking is not pursued then failure will result. It is to believe that there is a right and wrong way of being and doing, accompanied by degrees of brittleness and fragility. To be receptive, on the other hand, requires an ability to make creative leaps in order to reach out and assimilate new ideas and take risks. It enables the individual to empathise, to understand that there are other 'realities' in which children grow up, and brings with it awareness that one's own perspective is unique but not fixed.

In the context of behaviour management, the degree to which a teacher is receptive can have considerable implications. The unreceptive teacher is likely to find it difficult to take on board recommended management strategies for a child that clash with his/her own perception of the source of the child's needs (e.g. a self-esteem-raising programme if the teacher's perception is that the 'challenging' child is somehow undeserving of the teacher's positive attention). It is not unusual to find group 'closed' thinking within a staffroom (the opposite to receptivity), for example the labelling of all the siblings in a family accompanied by an unwillingness to believe that their behaviour can change for the better. Nor is it unusual for trainers to encounter some teachers who have been sent on their behaviour management courses and who see any such course as a waste of time because their way works for the 'normal kids'. This lack of openness can severely limit the teacher and be damaging for his/her students.

On the other hand, the receptive teacher is prepared to try new approaches and carries them out in a positive, energetic way and, by persisting with enthusiasm, brings about successful outcomes. Examples of receptivity can be found in the teacher who listens to and takes on board a parent's view on a child's behaviour; the teacher who is interested in innovative practice and actively looks to research for new approaches to improve students' outcomes; the teacher who uses a range of rewards and incentives and recognises that one size does not fit all; and the head teacher who appoints staff who will bring different perspectives in order to enrich the diversity of the school, making it more inclusive.

When receptiveness is absent, an educational psychologist's suggestions about strategies to use with a child may immediately be blocked without affording them reasonable consideration. The formal and informal labelling of children or classes/groups may be prevalent within the staffroom and harnessed with an unwillingness to believe that their behaviour can change for the better. A lack of receptivity leads teachers to believe that there are no benefits in attending behaviour management courses because they can only deliver teaching and manage the classroom in their habitual way.

---

**Ways to improve receptiveness**

- Be aware of your own patterns of thinking and behaving. Try to stand outside these and see how they may limit your understanding in certain areas.
- Set yourself the challenge of researching an approach or method of teaching that you previously dismissed without affording it due consideration.
- Make a determined effort to learn a new hobby/skill.
- Look for exceptions to the rule and try avoiding words like 'never' and 'always'.
- Reframe when considering a child's behaviour. What are the alternative perspectives on his/her needs? For example the child with ADHD may be described as creative, energetic and resourceful.
- Question stereotypes and be aware of your own prejudices and fixed attitudes.

---

The fourth tool, **resolute optimism,** is a state of mind that can be developed and nurtured. Resolute optimism is the determination to be and remain positive in the face of all the challenges that life presents. Bad things that happen are explained in terms of a constantly changing situation, which is like the Buddhist view (Yearley, 1997). Feeling positive generates increased energy resources that in themselves help to achieve successful outcomes. Resolute optimism is contagious and has an energising impact on those around you.

In the context of behaviour management, resolute optimism's importance is easily appreciated when observing a teacher's mode of operating in the classroom. The teacher who enters a classroom in a warm, appreciative and enthusiastic manner with obvious high expectation is likely to have this reflected back by the students. On the other hand the teacher entering the room with evident negative anticipation of what the lesson will be like will not give the students the positive, motivating messages they need.

***Ways to improve resolute optimism***

- Train yourself to adopt the 'glass half full' perspective and try to begin each day in a positive frame of mind.
- Take more exercise, as this helps to naturally release feel-good chemicals.
- Be aware of your energy levels and note the things that make you feel more energised, e.g. certain foods will give longer-term energy benefits.
- Note the impact that some people around you have on your energy levels and outlook. Analyse what it is about these people: are they upbeat and enthusiastic or are they critical and gloomy?
- Where other people bring your energy levels down, note that you can have an impact on this by introducing positive talk and outlooks.

These four personal tools or inner resources have been described separately but are in fact interdependent and connected in many ways. For example somebody who is resilient is inevitably going to be optimistic and will take full responsibility for finding solutions to difficulties by considering a range of options (receptiveness).

## Using the model

Essentially, successful behaviour management is hard work and there are no easy answers out there. Quick-fix strategies may sound appealing in the immediate term, but lasting success in behaviour management and long-term and meaningful changes can only really be achieved through enhanced self-knowledge and the development and deepening of the quality of relationships.

In the second part of this book, there is an opportunity to develop these ideas through engagement with six independent case studies. Each chapter (from Chapter 6 to Chapter 11) contains the story of a fictitious teacher, in which their personal and professional experiences are explored and analysed, revealing areas for development within a particular domain. Each of these chapters will offer the reader plentiful opportunity for self-reflection. Some readers will prefer to approach this as a private and individual exercise, while others may choose to incorporate the exercises into a group training activity. An alternative approach, and one that we have seen work very successfully, is a semi-formal peer coaching model.

## Peer coaching and the WBBM model

Peer coaching is a powerful tool that can be used to enhance the skills of teachers and implement change through an equitable relationship and mutual reciprocity (Joyce and Showers, 2006 [1995]). Our on-going research programme suggests that this approach can provide enormous benefits for teachers (and therefore learners) when used in conjunction with the WBBM model. Peer coaching helps teachers to develop their metacognitive skills, identify a focus for self-discovery and make progress towards successful outcomes through a series of professional conversations. Unlike some other forms of professional coaching, this method is based on a genuine partnership and provides a non-threatening model of personal and professional support because the approach is based on mutual reciprocity. J. Rogers (2004) describes the process as a 'dance of mutual influence and growth' (p. 23). There is no implicit assumption that one partner knows more or is more skilled than the other, as it is the process of questioning rather than instructing that is more likely to foster change and challenge self-limiting beliefs.

The CAB profile can be used as a helpful starting point for the coaching partnership, and the questions for reflection and goal-setting activities provided in Chapters 6 to 11 can be used to help facilitate the coaching sessions where appropriate. For those who are interested in pursuing this approach, there are some excellent books available on developing coaching skills and methods (for example Starr, 2003, or Whitworth et al., 1998).

# Part II

# Examining the pieces

# Chapter 6

# Grouping the yellow

## Psychology

People's behaviour makes sense if you think about it in terms of their goals, needs and motives.

(Thomas Mann, 1875–1955)

## The story of Belinda

Belinda teaches full time at a specialist unit for students who have been excluded from mainstream school on account of their behaviour. Belinda has responsibility for teaching a small group of six students, aged 12–13. She has developed an effective working relationship with four of the students but regularly experiences problems with two of the boys, Joseph and Toby. This is not an easy job and Belinda's manager really admires her commitment to these young people, her

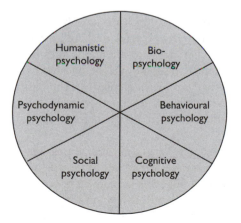

Figure 6.1 Yellow components.

resilience and her endless patience, but he can't help wondering whether Belinda, herself, sometimes incites or inflames the conflict, which seems to feature regularly in her classroom. For example, Belinda has been heard to make rather insensitive and thoughtless remarks on occasions, suggesting a lack of awareness. Read the following scenario to see if you agree with the manager's assessment of the situation:

Five of the six students are working separately at their tables, completing a piece of artwork. Joseph had worked hard for the first ten minutes but is now adopting his usual habit of wandering aimlessly around the room. Belinda tells him to return to his own table but he ignores her instruction. He takes a wet paintbrush from Tom's table and starts to flick water at the window. Tom swears loudly at Joseph and snatches back the brush. Belinda tells Joseph to return to his table, adding that he is 'far too old to be playing about with water'. Joseph immediately goes to the basin and starts to fill it with water. Belinda crosses the room, turns off the tap and gently guides Joseph away towards his table. Joseph suddenly resists and returns to the basin, this time turning the tap on full blast. He leaves the tap running while he goes to collect the paintbrushes and palettes from his table.

Belinda believes that Joseph is deliberately trying to annoy her in order to get a reaction so she tells herself to keep calm. She turns the tap off once more before the basin overflows and then stands in front of it, blocking Joseph's path as he returns a few moments later. Joseph tries to edge past her but Belinda stands firm with her arms crossed and shakes her head without making eye contact. Joseph hurls the brushes and palettes over her head and they land with a splash in the basin, soaking the back of Belinda's blouse. Joseph then walks out of the room, calling Belinda a 'stupid bitch' before slamming the door behind him.

Belinda lets out a long sigh and wipes her blouse with a paper towel. She is determined not to let this upset her. She has seen Joseph behave like this on countless occasions and knows he will probably return in a few minutes and act as though nothing has happened. Whenever he does this, Belinda tells him to go outside again until she gets an apology, but Joseph invariably refuses to accept responsibility for his actions or comply with this instruction.

She takes a deep breath and uses positive self-talk to help lift her spirits as she circulates amongst the other five students, who are working well, despite the commotion. She is pleased to see that Toby has finally got down to work and has produced a small but accurate image. This is a real achievement because it had taken him the first ten minutes to stop complaining and start painting in the first place. Belinda regularly gets frustrated with Toby because he wastes time and stubbornly refuses to start work at the beginning of many lessons. Belinda praises Toby and tells the others to stop what they are doing and look, as she holds his work aloft saying how wonderful it is. One of the girls sneers and says it is 'crap', and the others laugh. Toby snatches the paper from Belinda's hands, rips it up and kicks over his chair before he, too, storms out of the room.

Belinda calls after him, saying 'Don't be such a big baby! Come on, you need to come back and pick this litter up!' Belinda gets no response and she knows from experience that Toby will almost certainly be absent from school for the next few days.

## Questions to consider

- Why might Joseph often wander around the classroom instead of getting on with his work?
- Why did Joseph not comply with Belinda's instructions? Think of a number of possible explanations.
- Why do you think Joseph often acts 'as though nothing has happened' after an outburst like this?
- Think about times when you have:
  - put off doing something that you dreaded. (What were you afraid of?)
  - made excuses or feigned illness rather than tackle a challenge. (Do you still lack confidence in this area?)
  - felt as though everyone else around you was more skilful at something or more knowledgeable than you were. (Did you find some way of escaping?)
  - felt humiliated after a put-down. (How do you now protect yourself from further humiliation?)

- Now consider how Toby behaves at the beginning of lessons. Put yourself in his position and imagine his thoughts as Belinda explains the task ahead. Reflect on why Toby might feel this way about himself.
- Belinda was perplexed when Toby destroyed his work after her genuine and positive feedback. How would you explain this reaction to Belinda?
- Should Belinda now 'save face' by following Toby and insisting that he return immediately to clear up the paper? What are your reasons for thinking this?

Now read more about Belinda.

## More about Belinda

Belinda has held a number of part-time and temporary teaching positions in primary and secondary schools since starting a family of her own almost twenty years ago. She is an experienced and adaptable teacher who is enjoying her latest new challenge of working with excluded students. She is a warm and generous individual who, despite difficulties in her personal life, remains cheerful and upbeat most of the time. Belinda genuinely cares about the young people she teaches and is always willing to go out of her way for their benefit. Belinda puts a lot of energy and effort into making her lessons interesting and enjoyable. She is well organised and resourceful and her students have access to a rich and varied curriculum.

Belinda believes it is very important to develop and maintain positive relationships in the classroom and she works hard to achieve this. Although they don't always show it, the students appreciate her warmth and the interest she shows in them. She instinctively adopts a nurturing and motherly approach with her students and draws on the strategies she used with her own children when they were young (and before they rebelled during a very stormy and acrimonious period of adolescence!). She tends to use pet names such as 'Mr Grumpy' and uses humour to try to distract and deflect potential confrontation. Sometimes this approach works but, more often than not, her comments are perceived to be sarcastic or patronising and the aggression escalates as a result.

Belinda is an active supporter of the unit's positive behaviour management policy and she consciously uses praise in order to motivate and reward her students. She also maintains, and tells her students, that they always have a simple choice to make when it comes to behaviour. They can decide to behave reasonably and sensibly or they can choose to be rude and uncooperative. If they choose the latter, they must accept that there will be consequences.

Each day, when the students return home, there is a short staff meeting to discuss students' behaviour. Belinda contributes very little during these discussions, despite encouragement from her manager. When asked to comment on a student's uncontrolled outburst in order to analyse where things went wrong, Belinda typically says something like 'Oh, he was just in one of his funny little moods; nothing really caused it as such.'

Joseph has been diagnosed as having attention deficit hyperactivity disorder (ADHD), but Belinda has seen how he and his mother interact with each other during review meetings and she maintains that this 'label' is just an excuse for inadequate parenting skills. As far as Belinda is concerned, Joseph has learned to get his own way because his mother is not firm or assertive enough in her dealings with him. Belinda also has strong views on the use of Ritalin and maintains that 'naughty' children should not be drugged and sedated to make them more manageable.

Belinda has many strengths and is generally making a positive contribution to the lives of her students. She has good organisational skills (Chapter 8, the grey domain) and a high level of self-efficacy (Chapter 11, the pink domain). However, she does show a lack of psychological understanding at times in the way she responds to these emotionally vulnerable young people and this affects her relationship with them (especially Joseph and Toby). Belinda could enhance her practice in this respect through increased understanding and application of psychological theory.

## What do we mean by psychology?

Psychology is the study of human behaviour, so it is essential for teachers, as managers of behaviour, to have at the very least a basic understanding of the key psychological perspectives and their application in classroom practice. Unfortunately, the theoretical focus on the foundation disciplines (psychology, sociology and philosophy) has been largely driven out of initial teacher education owing to the emphasis on 'competence' and 'standards' models of teacher training in the UK. Although some teachers are naturally sensitive and intuitive to the psychological needs of their students, professional practice can be enhanced through increased breadth and depth of understanding in psychology.

## Psychology and the 'whole-brain' model

The branches of transpersonal and positive psychology are integral features of the WBBM approach. Transpersonal psychology is concerned with the processes that help teachers to experience a deeper or wider sense of who they are, enabling them to develop a sense of greater connection with the world around them, and positive psychology is concerned with the study of optimal human functioning. In the 'whole-brain' behaviour management (WBBM) model, this yellow psychology domain is made up of components that explore six other perspectives on behaviour that, when considered together, can provide the teacher with a more rounded understanding of student behaviour. These are:

- bio-psychology;
- behavioural psychology;
- cognitive behavioural psychology;
- social psychology;
- psychodynamic psychology;
- humanistic psychology.

## Bio-psychology

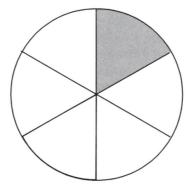

This segment considers biological or neurological explanations for difficult behaviour. The biological perspective has, in recent history, been approached with extreme caution by educationists who acknowledged the adverse and limiting effects that such labelling could have on pupils' attainment and teachers' expectations. In other words, if we perceive challenging behaviour as something that is biologically determined (a trait or predisposition that children are born with) then this may lead us to conclude that there is little we can do about it. Another caveat associated with this model is that it implies that these different ways of thinking and behaving are 'impaired' or 'abnormal' and thus require interventions that make the individual fit in with our culturally determined notion of 'normality'. Finally, it is important to bear in mind that, although medical labels can be useful, they usually represent a spectrum of characteristics and there is often a huge variation between individuals and the ways in which they are affected by various conditions (for example autistic spectrum disorder).

Having noted this, developments in neuroimaging (including scanning techniques that can monitor blood flow and metabolism in different parts of the brain) have led to huge advances in understanding and have revived interest in this perspective. For example, neuroscientists have discovered links between conditions such as ADHD and structural patterns in different regions of the brain, which help to explain the biological basis of certain behaviours and provide scientific evidence to contradict previous assumptions about the condition being caused by learned behaviour and/or inadequate parenting skills. Studies have also identified a deficiency in levels of dopamine and noradrenaline (neurotransmitters known to act as powerful regulators and integrators of different aspects of brain functions) in individuals with ADHD.

Belinda is dismissive of Joseph's ADHD diagnosis. She has read a few newspaper articles and watched TV programmes about the disorder but remains sceptical. She refuses to accept ADHD as a bona fide neurological condition and clings to the theory that 'so-called' ADHD is a convenient excuse for inadequate parenting skills. A greater awareness and understanding of ADHD could influence Belinda's relationship with Joseph (and his parents) and help her to manage his behaviour more effectively in the classroom.

ADHD is typically characterised by a collection of symptoms for which there may be several different causes. Joseph's attention difficulties (including his wandering around the room and flitting from one activity to another) may well arise from dysfunction of the prefrontal cortex. Belinda needs to understand that Joseph's problem is not that he cannot attend, but rather that he attends to everything and is easily distracted by external stimuli, which affects his ability to sustain attention. When Belinda makes the reference to 'playing about with water', she inadvertently focuses Joseph's attention on this and he immediately goes to the basin and turns on the tap. Through a more conscious use of directional language (for example 'Joseph, I need you to show me your finished painting'), Belinda might have distracted Joseph in a more positive way. Belinda might also reconsider her seating plan and provide a quiet area away from distractions, allow Joseph to wear earphones when working independently, ensure that she makes eye contact when speaking to him and set him short tasks with regular breaks between activities.

Belinda interpreted Joseph's behaviour with the water as an attempt to wind her up and she dealt with this perceived threat by keeping calm and using positive self-talk to keep her emotions in check. Had Belinda understood more about Joseph's condition, she might also have recognised this response as a lack of impulse control, which is caused by difficulties with the brain's executive functions. Linked to this, Joseph often acts on a whim, without considering the consequences or using what he has learned from past mistakes. The difficulty he has in using hindsight (retrospective functioning) and foresight (prospective functioning) is frustrating for Belinda as she assumes he hasn't listened to her or is being deliberately defiant, but this characteristic is related to Joseph's short-term memory impairment. People with ADHD also have difficulties in regulating their emotions (see Chapter 10) and, in this example, Joseph displays emotional impulsiveness in the way that he inexplicably storms out of the room when Belinda prevents him from washing the brushes.

Finally, Belinda's fixed perception of Joseph's mother's parenting skills is almost bound to affect the quality of the home–school relationship. Belinda may even come across as unsupportive and judgemental in her interactions with Joseph's mother. She may be adding to his mother's guilt by making subjective and unhelpful remarks about the use of medication. Greater insight into research findings might help Belinda to understand how stimulant medications work as a chemical facilitator and to appreciate how Joseph's ADHD may have caused an ineffective parenting style (through exhaustion, frustration and demoralisation) rather than the other way round.

***Bio-psychology: self-reflection exercise***

How much do you know and understand about the following conditions? Where did your information come from? How recent was the research underpinning this source?

- Attention deficit hyperactivity disorder (ADHD)
- Autistic spectrum disorder (ASD)
- Asperger syndrome (AS)
- Tourette syndrome
- Obsessive compulsive disorder (OCD)
- Oppositional defiance disorder (ODD)
- Dyslexia
- Dyspraxia
- Dyscalculia

Why not set yourself the target of updating your knowledge about these conditions (including the way that they are related or connected)?

## Behavioural psychology

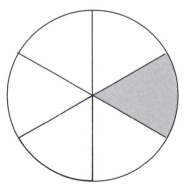

Behavioural psychology, or 'behaviourism', is a psychological perspective that grew out of scientific experimentation and observation of animal behaviour in the laboratory. Behavioural psychologists propound the theory that behaviour can be observed and analysed scientifically and that behaviour is learned and can therefore be unlearned. In order to help an individual 'unlearn' an unwanted behaviour and replace it with a new and more appropriate one, it is necessary first to identify and then 'manipulate' or make changes to the stimulus (antecedent) and/or the response (consequence). In this way, the behaviour can be shaped, conditioned and ultimately modified by repeatedly (if necessary) applying positive or negative reinforcement. A simple example of this might be:

- A student calls out answers in class because he has **learned** that this is the way to get attention from the teacher. Even though it is negative attention, it is still attention!
- The teacher wants to **change** this aspect of the student's behaviour.
- The teacher changes her usual **response** (instead of getting impatient and cross with the student whenever he calls out the answer, the teacher decides to keep her attention on students who have put their hands up).
- The student is getting no attention and so eventually raises his hand. The teacher notices and praises the student for following the class rule (**positive reinforcement**).
- This process is **repeated** a few times.
- The student's behaviour is eventually **modified** and he learns to put his hand up in future to gain the teacher's attention.
- The unwanted behaviour (calling out) is **extinguished**.

Alternatively, the teacher might have manipulated the stimulus instead of the consequence. She might have decided to change the way that she asks questions to the class. Rather than inviting any student to answer her questions by raising their hands she might have chosen instead to name individual students to respond.

Behaviourist methods are a common feature of most classrooms. Teachers routinely use praise, stickers, stamps, house points and various privileges to reward (and therefore reinforce) the behaviour that they want from their students. Conversely, they may verbally rebuke, isolate students or withdraw certain privileges from them in order to punish (and therefore deter) inappropriate behaviour. These are examples of shaping behaviour by manipulating the consequence. Alternatively, by seating students in particular ways (such as rows as opposed to tables or in boy/girl order) teachers deliberately 'manipulate' the antecedent in order to modify and improve the students' learning behaviour. In most schools today (with the promotion of positive behaviour management programmes) there is a will to place greater emphasis on positive reinforcement rather than punishment.

In many circumstances this simple behaviourist approach, which is a fundamental principle of animal training techniques, is found to be effective. However, managing children's behaviour is a far more complex affair than training puppies or mice, and there are a number of restraints that can limit the effectiveness of this approach in the classroom:

- We may be able to observe students' behaviour but we cannot observe students' thoughts (including their motives for behaving in certain ways).
- This perspective takes no account of cognitive or psychodynamic reasons for the behaviour.
- The principle of 'learned behaviour' fails to acknowledge that there may be biological or neurological reasons for a student to behave in particular ways.
- Rewards and consequences will only be effective if they have currency and meaning for the student.
- Some intended rewards may actually deter the desired behaviour, and some intended sanctions may encourage unwanted behaviour to continue.

Although it is unlikely that Belinda would be able to put a name to her methods, she is heavily influenced by the behaviourist perspective. She frequently uses praise and encouragement in a conscious way, as she believes that this helps to improve the students' behaviour, and she actively supports all aspects of the unit's positive behaviour policy. Behaviourist methods, by their very nature, tend to be systematic, highly structured and consistently applied. Although this can be safe and reassuring for students, it can also create more problems than it solves if systems are so inflexible that they fail to take account of students' complex emotional needs and individual circumstances. For example, Belinda has a policy of sharing examples of good work with the rest of the group. Her underlying belief is that this approach will make the students feel proud of their achievements and therefore be motivated to repeat this level of effort in future lessons. What she fails to appreciate is that students like Toby (whose self-esteem is so damaged) cannot cope emotionally with this type of public praise and he therefore reacts aggressively or withdraws completely by running out of the room. Belinda might have avoided this scenario by choosing instead to have a private word with Toby after the lesson to acknowledge her admiration for his efforts.

Belinda also applies consequences in a rigid way because she strongly believes that her students are capable of and therefore able to choose the 'correct' behaviour at all times. This assumption fails to acknowledge the fact that the students may not have developed the necessary level of emotional literacy (see Chapter 10) to be able to regulate their strong emotions and act in the measured and rational way that Belinda expects. When Belinda's own children were teenagers, their frustration at her apparent inability to tune into their emotional needs and show understanding towards them as young people resulted in daily rows and periods of estrangement.

---

### Behavioural psychology: self-reflection exercise

Think about the sanctions that you apply in order to deter unwanted behaviour from your students. Are there some that are more likely to produce the desired effect than others? Consider why this might be the case.

What motivates you to work hard and achieve things? What is it that encourages you to 'do the right thing'? Is it the prospect of a tangible reward (e.g. financial gain or prize)? Are you motivated by symbolic rewards such as an award or certificate? Perhaps it is special treats or privileges that spur you on? Is social approval the thing that influences you most or drives you forward? Or do you try hard just to prove something to yourself? Now think about the range of students in your class and the types of rewards that you currently make available. Could this be a reason why some rewards are less effective with some students?

Informative reinforcers are said to be more effective than affirmative ones. When praising students, how often do you remember to provide informative feedback, for example 'You remembered to say "Thank you" that time. Well done'?

---

## Cognitive behavioural psychology

The cognitive behavioural perspective, which developed in response to the limitations of behaviourist theory, as discussed in the previous

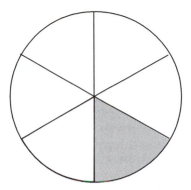

section, is based on the premise that it is our thoughts that ultimately determine our feelings and behaviour (a key principle of the WBBM model). When thoughts are irrational or in some way dysfunctional, then behaviour difficulties can manifest themselves. According to this perspective, therefore, the way to change problem behaviour is to change the maladaptive thought processes that are actually driving it. This is usually considered to be the remit of psychologists, self-help gurus and therapeutic clinicians, all of whom promote methods such as cognitive behaviour therapy (CBT), rational emotive therapy and solution-focused therapy to help address moderate to severe 'problem' behaviours such as irrational fear, eating disorders, social anxiety, depression and psychoses. However, this perspective is also becoming more influential in the classroom as teachers increasingly recognise the benefits of addressing behaviour problems by encouraging students to examine behavioural interpretations and their motives for thinking, feeling and acting in particular ways. A good example of this is the growth in anger management and anti-bullying programmes in schools.

In the scenario above, the student Toby shows signs of learned helplessness, a concept described by Abramson *et al.* (1978). In other words, Toby has learned, through experience, to believe that whatever he does is futile so he gives up trying. What Toby will remember from the art lesson described earlier is that he was teased and laughed at by his classmates for his efforts. This will reinforce the view he holds of himself as a failure and overshadow Belinda's appreciation and positive comments. Seligman (1998) would say that Toby has a pessimistic 'explanatory style'. He sees events as being 'internal, universal and permanent' – 'I am rubbish at Art and always will be!'

Seligman suggests that students like Toby can learn to change the way they interpret events through a cognitive behavioural approach.

Teachers who adopt a cognitive behavioural approach are likely to encourage their students to use:

- self-rating scales that reflect perceptions about their own behaviour;
- collaborative target-setting exercises and self-monitoring procedures;
- 'think sheets' to encourage them to reflect upon their behaviour and its impact on others;
- sociometric exercises to provide an insight into the students' view of others and their perception of relationships within the classroom;
- brief solution-focused therapy to help students reframe their thoughts and adopt a more optimistic outlook (see Chapter 11);
- restorative justice approaches that encourage students to build empathy with those they have bullied, hurt or abused.

Whereas the behaviourist approach relies upon extrinsic factors to 'control' student behaviour (rewards and sanctions in all their various forms), the cognitive behavioural perspective is concerned with developing intrinsic controls such as emotional literacy, coping skills (self-efficacy) and self-management. In short, cognitive behavioural methods aim to encourage greater student independence and self-control grounded in empathy and moral ethics with less reliance on extrinsic systems of rewards and sanctions. In the scenario provided, Belinda might have adopted a cognitive behavioural approach when Joseph took Tom's paintbrush without asking or when the female student made a disparaging remark about Toby's work. In neither case did Belinda follow this up by exploring the motive and discussing the impact of the behaviour with the students concerned. Belinda tends to avoid this type of discussion, as she doesn't believe in analysing or dwelling on behaviour. The fact that Toby regularly misses periods of school after an emotional outburst is bound to have a detrimental effect on his social as well as his academic development. Belinda could perhaps support him, using a cognitive behavioural approach, such as mentoring, in which Toby is helped to explore his maladaptive thoughts and learn to cope when facing similar circumstances, in different and more productive ways.

> **Cognitive behavioural psychology:**
> **self-reflection exercise**
>
> What cognitive behavioural influences are included in your teaching methods? What are the direct and indirect benefits of this approach for your students and for you as their teacher?
>
> How confident are you that your class would behave well if you had to leave them unsupervised for a few minutes? Do you always get good reports when they are taught by a trainee teacher or an unfamiliar supply or substitute teacher? What might be the reason for your conclusions?
>
> Think of one whole-class initiative that you could introduce to enhance your students' self-management skills. Think of one student who might benefit from a cognitive-type approach to help change his/her maladaptive and limiting self-beliefs into more positive thoughts. How might you go about implementing a programme of support for him/her?

## Social psychology

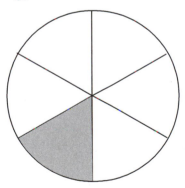

As already outlined in Chapter 3, social psychology is concerned with theoretical explanations about the nature and causes of human social behaviour. It seeks to understand and explain how human individuals operate in a social context: how they perceive, relate to and communicate with others and how they exert influence (or are influenced by others). These are all vitally important aspects of knowledge for the classroom practitioner, and much of the teacher's role is concerned with applied social psychology.

Within this branch of psychology, theories of attribution (e.g. Heider, 1958; Kelley, 1967) can help to explain the way that we perceive and interpret the causality of behaviour. For example, Belinda demonstrates what psychologists call an external attribution style whenever she assigns the causality of an event to an external force (Joseph is a difficult student because his mother is too lenient with him). In 1985, Croll and Moses conducted a survey of over 400 primary school teachers. When asked to give their explanations for the behaviour problems of children in their classes, 66 per cent attributed them to home circumstances, 30 per cent to 'within-child' factors and less than 4 per cent to school or teacher factors. However, Miller *et al.*'s (2000) study of pupils' causal attributions for difficult behaviour in a UK secondary school found that pupils generally attributed poor behaviour to school and teacher factors. It is important for teachers to acknowledge that there are these conflicting attributions and different perceptions of reality.

Belinda is never very willing to talk about or analyse her students' behaviour. Her philosophy is 'What's done is done' and it is always best to move on. This shows **resilience** on Belinda's part but also a lack of **responsibility** and **receptivity**. This has been noted by her manager, who has tried on several occasions to encourage Belinda to explore the source of conflict in her lessons. An understanding of the theory of transactional analysis (see Chapters 3 and 9) might enable Belinda to encourage more harmonious student interaction within the group and throw some light on the reasons why the comments she makes to students sometimes (unintentionally) provoke them and seem to inflame emotional outbursts. This includes her use of irony and pet names such as 'Mr Grumpy' or 'My little ray of sunshine' which cause embarrassment and encourage merciless teasing within the group. A fundamental knowledge of social psychology can help to underpin the teaching of social skills, emotional literacy and cooperative learning within the classroom and enable teachers to deal more effectively with instances of aggression, and bullying, sexism and racism. Persuasion techniques, mediation skills and conflict resolution can also be enhanced through a better understanding of social psychology.

---

### Social psychology: self-reflection exercise

Try to be more aware of how you attribute behaviour. Do you rely mainly on external or within-child explanations? Try to perceive the problem behaviour from the student's perspective and from the student's parent or carer's perspective. Do you see a different picture?

How satisfied are you with the social ethos in your classroom? Do the students function as a cohesive group? Are there exclusive cliques? How welcome are new students made to feel? Are you aware of students who are socially isolated? Do you regularly find yourself having to deal with squabbles and arguments?

Spend some time observing the students during unstructured times (such as break), with a focus on their social interaction. How do they initiate play, contact and conversations? What causes conflict and how is it resolved? What does all this reveal? Are there implications for teaching here?

How do you currently teach social (interpersonal) skills? Is this something that is explicit in your teaching? Think of the ways that these skills can be modelled to the students.

---

## Psychodynamic psychology

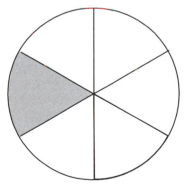

The psychodynamic perspective of behaviour (which has its roots in Freudian theory and is therefore sometimes referred to as neo-Freudian) asserts that emotional and behavioural difficulties are driven by unconscious phenomena that originate in the early stages of child development. According to this perspective, early painful memories remain with us but in order to protect and defend the ego (and the individual's sense of worth) they are banished to the unconscious mind and kept there by forces referred to as 'defence mechanisms'. When individuals experience anxiety-producing thoughts and feared impulses, this acts as a trip-wire that triggers the defence mechanisms and stops the painful memories from re-entering the consciousness. Sometimes students behave in ways that seem inexplicable to the teacher, and it may be helpful under these circumstances to consider whether these behaviours may be defence mechanisms that are covering deep-seated anxieties. Some examples of defence mechanisms are outlined below.

---

### Ego defence mechanisms

- Denial: A student complains that 'This work is boring and babyish' when in reality he finds it too difficult and this fact is causing him distress.
- Displacement: A student kicks over a chair when she is upset by a teacher's remark.
- Intellectualisation: Even when told to stop, a student keeps adding more and more unnecessary details to his work to avoid the threat of being told it is incorrect.
- Projection: A student becomes frustrated and calls the teacher a 'stupid idiot' when she just doesn't understand what the teacher is trying to tell her.
- Rationalisation: A student swears on his mother's life that he was never told about the rule that he has just broken (and for which he will be punished). He convinces himself that this is true even though it isn't.
- Reaction formation: A timid student attaches himself to loud and brash peers even though they frighten him, or a student who is mistrustful of adults is forward and over-familiar with visiting professionals.
- Regression: A student sucks his thumb or has a temper tantrum when faced with conflict.

---

Belinda sees examples of this type of behaviour on a regular basis but it leaves her baffled and unsure of how to deal with it. The students can't seem to explain themselves either (because they are not consciously aware of the causes), so situations are left unresolved. If a student displays regressive behaviour (such as crawling under a table and refusing to come out), Belinda tries to 'jolly' them or, if that doesn't work, she will attempt to shame them out of their mood by drawing attention to their immaturity and 'babyishness'. However, according to the psychodynamic perspective, this type of behaviour is indicative of a deep insecurity and the student is communicating the need for safety by reverting to an earlier stage of development. This is the theory behind the Nurture Group movement that was pioneered by Marion Bennathan and Marjorie Boxall (1996), which aims to support children and young people with complex needs by enabling them to revisit earlier stages of emotional development in a safe, structured and nurturing learning environment.

If children or young people have been let down or rejected by significant adults in their early years, they may protect themselves by habitually entering into a process of 'testing' new adult figures in their lives. They may behave in a highly provocative or unreasonable manner to trigger the 'inevitable' rejection (before they become too attached to the person and suffer even more hurt as a result). Having an understanding of this can be helpful to teachers, who may otherwise take this kind of reaction personally.

---

### Psychodynamic psychology: self-reflection exercise

Consider the defence mechanisms described above. Which of these behaviours have you come across in your teaching experience? How did you interpret them at the time? How did you respond to them?

How do you prepare students for times of transition such as moving from one class to another? Are there some students (with insecure attachment) who might need a different approach in order to help them cope?

Some teachers find that using metaphors in literature, circle time or drama activities can help troubled students to safely recognise and begin to understand their own confused emotions (see for example Sunderland, 2000). Is this an approach that you have used or might consider using?

## Humanistic psychology

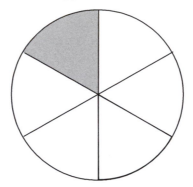

Humanistic psychology developed during the 1950s and 1960s as a reaction against behavioural and psychodynamic schools of psychology. The essence of the humanistic perspective is that individuals function as whole beings with thoughts and feelings and a basic drive for learning new things. According to the fathers of humanistic psychology, Abraham Maslow (whose maxim was quoted at the beginning of Chapter 1) and Carl Rogers, we learn best when our basic needs are met and when we feel good about ourselves.

Learning is an emotional business that requires confidence and the willingness to take risks. Toby resists or avoids tasks altogether because he is afraid of failure and criticism. Belinda notices that Toby hangs back, and interprets this behaviour as wilful stubbornness and an attempt to disrupt her carefully planned lesson. Her irritation draws more attention towards him and he withdraws even further. Belinda knows about the importance of self-esteem for learning but fails to recognise this as the cause of Toby's behaviour in the heat of the moment.

Self-esteem is not a fixed state but is one that fluctuates (some theorists argue that because it is not a singular entity it should be referred to in the plural – self-esteems). Students with social, emotional and behavioural difficulties (including those with ADHD) have probably spent a lifetime listening to corrections, reprimands and expressions of disappointment. They therefore find it difficult to accept praise because there is such a mismatch between the message they are being given and the view they have learned to hold of themselves (see Chapter 11). Praise may be rejected by contradicting the teacher or (as in the case of Toby) destroying work in a public show. Toby could not cope with being singled out and praised in such a public manner and as soon as the female student made the remark he was expecting (the one that conformed to his self-image) he reacted emotionally.

Teachers who use humanistic approaches to teaching place a great deal of emphasis on enhancing their students' emotional development and self-esteem. They tend to be child-centred and encourage participatory and self-directed methods of learning that relate to the students' interests and lives and therefore more effectively motivate them.

---

**Humanistic psychology: self-reflection exercise**

Think of a time when your self-esteem was really high. What did this feel like? What caused you to feel this way about yourself? What did it enable you to achieve?

Now consider a time when your self-esteem was low. What effect did this have on your life, relationships and achievements?

Can you think of a student who is reluctant to take risks, is fearful of change and makes self-disparaging remarks? Why not make a point of giving this student 'psychological strokes' (see Chapter 3) or your focused attention to help raise his/her self-esteem?

Now think of a student who frequently boasts and shows off in class. This type of behaviour often characterises 'false high esteem'. This student is likely to be in need of strokes too!

---

In this chapter, we have taken a brief look at six different psychological perspectives. Most effective teachers use a combination of these influences in their practice in recognition of the fact that behaviour is complex and can rarely be traced to a single cause. Most experts agree that most challenging behaviour can only be reliably explained by considering a biopsychosocial theory, which takes account of the interaction between biological, psychological and social factors.

## A review of Belinda – adopting a 'whole-brain' approach

Belinda's six students are all working independently at their tables, completing a piece of artwork. Joseph has been engrossed in the task for almost half an hour, which is unusual for him, as he is normally distracted and off-task after a few minutes. Belinda had been monitoring Joseph's behaviour patterns for a few days and she had noticed that he seemed to have 'a window of efficacy' at this time of day, linked to the timing of his medication for ADHD. She has also moved Joseph's table away from the window after their chat about what helped him to concentrate better.

The morning started well with a circle time activity in which the students openly discussed the effects of name calling. Belinda had been sceptical when her manager initially suggested the idea of attending training in this approach but now she is enthusiastic and convinced about the benefits it brings to her classroom. During the course of this morning's circle time, Belinda was taken aback when one of the students, Danny, revealed that it made him feel 'shamed' when Belinda called him 'silly sausage' in front of the others. Belinda immediately recalled an occasion when Danny had suddenly attacked another pupil for 'smirking' at him and she apologised for making him feel this way. Together, the class decided on some basic ground rules about name calling and now they are designing posters and images to express their ideas.

Toby had shown some reluctance as usual at the outset of the activity, but, once Belinda had spent a few minutes reassuring him and talking through some ideas, he was willing to try and has produced a very fine piece of work. Belinda circulates the room giving private encouragement and informative feedback. She points out to Toby what she likes about his poster but does not engulf him with praise, as she knows he finds this difficult at the moment.

Noticing that Joseph has lost concentration and is now beginning to distract Danny, Belinda suggests that he might like to take his work to show the unit manager. This is a strategy that the staff have worked out between them and it works well for students like Joseph who are especially motivated by social approval.

Table 6.1 Psychology self-review

| What aspect of psychology do I want to improve? | What can I do to improve this? | How will this impact on my management of behaviour? |
| --- | --- | --- |
| | | |

# Chapter 7

# Grouping the blue

## Knowledge

> Whereof one cannot speak, thereof one should not talk.
>
> (Ludwig Wittgenstein, 1889–1951)

## The story of Adrian

Adrian is a newly qualified teacher employed on a temporary contract (to cover a maternity leave) in an inner city primary school. He has been teaching at this school for less than four weeks and his contextual knowledge of the school, its policies and systems is less than secure, as he has had no formal induction training. He is gradually getting to know his class of 7- to 8-year-olds but he has only a limited understanding of the specific learning and emotional needs of individual students. Adrian is an arts graduate and feels rather

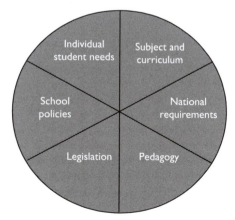

*Figure 7.1* Blue components.

insecure about the teaching of science and technology. It is within these areas of the curriculum that he is experiencing most difficulty with behaviour management. Read the description below to gain more insight into the nature of Adrian's difficulties:

It is the Tuesday afternoon of Adrian's fourth week at the school and he has finally got round to delivering his first science lesson. Recently, some of the children had begun to ask him when they would be having science and, having found reasons not to teach the subject over the past three weeks, he realises that he can no longer justify his avoidance. According to the (regular) class teacher's planning file, the scheme of work for this term requires him to teach the class about the forces of gravity and resistance alongside the development and assessment of the children's observational and investigative skills.

Thinking about his class of twenty-eight students, Adrian has attempted to prepare for this science lesson, but his lack of scientific understanding, together with his increasing self-doubt and frustration at his limitations, has become a major barrier to him being able to plan an effective learning experience. During the previous evening, Adrian had vacillated between various approaches and lesson structures until finally abandoning his planning in disgust. The result is that now Adrian faces the afternoon lacking the necessary expertise, knowledge and understanding and without a clear structure for the lesson. He has collected together a vast range of equipment for the children to use in carrying out investigative activities.

He begins the lesson well (but with a gnawing anxiety about the outcome), leading the class in a mind-mapping exercise which enables them to share with him and one another all that they already know about forces. There is some good whole-class discussion in which the pupils give examples of forces from their everyday experience, but it also raises a number of misconceptions, which Adrian fails to follow up, owing to his own uncertainty. Adrian also has to speak sharply to a couple of boys who start to push and pull each other quite roughly when these terms are introduced.

Adrian swiftly moves the class into the practical part of the lesson. He asks them to get into groups of four, but does not specify how they are to do this, and then tells them that, in their groups, they have fifteen minutes to carry out the task of selecting equipment from the tables set up in each corner of the room. Once they have selected equipment they have to make a model that demonstrates a force in action and then they must prepare themselves to present their model to the rest of the class, explaining what is happening. Initially, he feels some relief that he has got the students' thinking about forces well under way and hopes that the task will somehow meet some of the criteria for this programme of study.

Within two minutes of the students going into their groups, Adrian sees chaos erupting at several points in the room. There is obvious excitement at the opportunity to 'play' with this range of equipment, but this is accompanied by anxiety for some students who obviously feel insecure owing to the lack of clarity and clear structure. There are evident power-struggle arguments going on between certain individuals. Some students seem to freeze as the noise level swiftly escalates, and it becomes evident to Adrian that this approach to investigating forces is so different to anything the children have experienced before that they are unable to cope with it. Five minutes into the practical activity, a scuffle breaks out in one group and Adrian has to physically intervene to prevent harm. This results in two boys having to be removed from the classroom.

## Questions to consider

- What range of emotions might students experience when they have a new teacher?
- What information about the class was not considered when Adrian planned this lesson?
- What is the essential information that teachers new to a school need to know in order to help them manage behaviour effectively?
- What are the advantages and disadvantages of allowing pupils to group themselves for an activity? What variables might you need to consider in assessing the impact of this approach (e.g. maturity level)?
- What else could Adrian have done to make his science planning more effective?

- Reflecting on your own experience, is there a curriculum area (or aspect of a subject) that seems to be the context for more behaviour problems?

Now read more about Adrian below.

## More about Adrian

Adrian graduated from university with a good degree in English literature. At this stage in his life, he was unsure about the career direction he wanted to pursue, but when he saw an advertisement for a temporary teaching assistant in a local primary school it immediately appealed to him. Although the position was not particularly well paid, it was close to his home and Adrian felt that the experience of working in a school might help him decide whether or not a teaching career would suit him. Adrian quickly developed a warm and empathic relationship with the children he supported and was praised by his colleagues for his natural flair and enthusiasm. The head teacher was delighted with Adrian's contribution to the school and extended his contract for another term. After only a few months in the job, Adrian (with support and encouragement from his mentor) applied for a place on a post-graduate teacher training course at his local university and was accepted. Adrian subsequently achieved qualified teacher status but then made the decision to defer applying for his first teaching position. He decided that, while he was still young, he wanted to spend some time travelling and seeing the world before settling into his career. Eighteen months later, Adrian returned home but has since been unable to secure a permanent teaching post. In the meantime, he gained some teaching experience and attempted to increase his chances of finding permanent employment by undertaking casual work as a supply (substitute) teacher, through an agency. He has recently been appointed to this temporary post, covering the maternity leave of a teacher of a class of 7- to 8-year-olds in an inner city school.

Adrian is the youngest of three siblings from a very creative and artistic family. His father is a professional actor, and his mother, who works as an alternative therapist, left a career in nursing to pursue a more holistic approach to healing. His brother is a musician, and his sister lectures at art college. He grew up in a home where creativity was highly valued and encouraged, while some aspects of the traditional sciences were questioned. As a result, Adrian has many strengths within the arts but finds himself questioning aspects of traditional scientific knowledge and research methods.

Adrian feels reasonably confident about his ability to teach most aspects of the primary curriculum. However, it was during his post-graduate training that he realised he struggled with many aspects of science and technology teaching. He was aware that he did not feel as interested in or passionate about this area of the curriculum, but was unable to overcome this personal resistance. The post-graduate training route did not allow for in-depth study of each curriculum subject, as it was predominantly school based. Therefore, the gaps in Adrian's knowledge and understanding were largely hidden.

As a classroom practitioner, Adrian is developing good communication skills. He is able to build warm and productive relationships with the students and is naturally inclusive in his approach. He understands the importance of sound preparation and lesson organisation and is able to structure his delivery accordingly. He is skilled in being able to motivate and enthuse students in those aspects of the curriculum he is most interested in. In some lessons, for example English, drama, music and art, he seems to be able to captivate the children and, because they enjoy these learning experiences, they are cooperative and well behaved. At other times, they can be rude and challenging, leaving Adrian feeling that he is losing his authority.

Adrian is having mixed experience when it comes to behaviour management. His skills and confidence levels seem to fluctuate during the course of a day. The children are never quite sure what to expect and neither is Adrian.

## What do we mean by knowledge?

This 'blue' domain within the wheel of competencies is concerned with a whole range of knowledge and understanding that collectively enables a teacher to fulfil his/her role effectively. By 'knowledge' we refer not only to subject and curriculum knowledge but also to an entire raft of understanding that includes a critical awareness of pedagogical theory and practice, familiarisation with macro and micro policy matters and processes, a working knowledge of key legislative implications, and specific and background knowledge of individual students' interests, needs and circumstances (including cultural and linguistic needs).

Each of these components is now explored in more detail below.

## Subject and curriculum knowledge

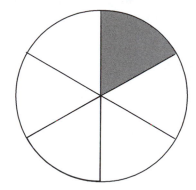

This component has different implications for teachers depending on the age group of the students that they teach. For those who teach in the early years or primary phases this component clearly requires a breadth as well as a depth of curriculum knowledge encompassing the basic concepts that underpin all future learning in each subject discipline. An example of this is teaching young children one-to-one correspondence in counting as a prerequisite for all future mathematical understanding. The effective teaching of such key concepts is crucial in ensuring a student's understanding at all stages of his/her education and thereby limiting the likelihood of frustration manifested through challenging behaviour.

This component may appear to have less relevance for the secondary phase teacher, who is usually a specialist in a particular discipline anyway, but there are important considerations. For example the comprehensive school system requires the specialist to be able to deliver the subject at a number of different levels. Within a single class, the range of understanding may stretch from students with significant barriers to learning to those with a high level of conceptual awareness (gifted). At secondary level there is often an expectation that staff will teach or cover subjects that lie outside their specific area of expertise. This is particularly true for supply or substitute teachers, who may find that they regularly face challenges within several components of this domain.

In Adrian's case, his strengths are within the arts and he has been avoiding the teaching of science until it is no longer feasible to do so. This reluctance on Adrian's part stems from a combination of unconscious conditioning during his formative years, which has led to a disassociation with science and a general insecurity and lack of preparedness about teaching the subject. Adrian realises that he needs to address this gap and spends a considerable amount of time thinking about how to deliver this lesson on forces, but his own lack of understanding is the significant barrier. Adrian desperately wants to make a good impression at the school and is therefore reluctant to draw attention to his weakness by asking for help and advice, so he tries to cover it up by delivering the lesson in a way that he believes will avoid exposing his inadequacy.

Having adequate subject knowledge is essential for effective teaching and learning, but in this context more specifically for effective behaviour management. In order to deliver a lesson with confidence (meeting the learning needs of every student at whatever level), teachers need to feel secure about their own depth of knowledge and understanding in the particular aspect in which they are directing the learning. Anything less than adequate knowledge will inevitably impact on the quality of delivery and the teacher's ability to manage the lesson.

---

### Subject and curriculum knowledge: self-reflection exercise

Do you think that students are able to sense a teacher's insecurity about subject knowledge?

Have you ever attended a course or presentation in which it was fairly clear that the person delivering it was less than well informed? How did this affect the behaviour and dynamic of the group? What emotions did you, as a learner (or recipient), experience?

Reflect on your own teaching practice. Which curriculum subject, lesson or course do you feel most enthusiastic, competent and confident about teaching? Now consider the behaviour of students in your 'favourite' lesson. Is there a positive connection between the two? Do you feel more confident because the students are well behaved or are they well behaved because you feel more confident?

Now think of a particular occasion when you have had to teach a lesson and felt out of your comfort zone because of a lack of subject knowledge or relevant experience. What strategies did you draw upon to enable you to get through the experience? Were there other strategies you could have employed to make the lesson more successful?

Are there any areas of the curriculum that you are required to teach but that you feel insecure about? Where does this insecurity come from? Can you identify a source? Can you pinpoint a specific event that may have led to this self-perception or disassociation?

Do you feel able to challenge this self-perception? Is there anything stopping you being receptive to a different view of yourself? Do you take responsibility for your own professional development?

What do you believe is needed for you to feel more confident and knowledgeable in this area? For example are there courses that you could access? Are there colleagues or other professionals whom you could observe or ask for support from?

## Knowledge of national requirements (for the delivery and assessment of the curriculum)

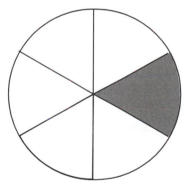

National requirements for the delivery and assessment of the curriculum are laid down by statute and government regulations that shape educational policy and practice. For example, there may be an explicit and nationally agreed requirement for all teachers to teach the same curriculum content to particular age groups, adopt similar methods in delivering this content and assess specific skills and knowledge using the same assessment tools on specific dates.

As a result of statute, teachers are required to work within such national frameworks and are expected to keep up to date with all modifications to such requirements. If they fail to do so, they may face disciplinary action or even legal repercussions. Teachers who are confident in their knowledge and understanding of the curriculum tend to be far more creative in structuring and planning their teaching. They are able to take more risks in bringing the content to life for their students and in so doing are more able to enthuse and engage. Teachers who have a less-than-adequate grasp of the content and structure of the curriculum will struggle to understand the deeper structure of what they have to impart and inevitably feel less confident. Being less sure about content (and meeting the legal requirements) impacts on teacher confidence and results in less creativity and risk taking.

This component is generally monitored by performance management and formal inspection processes (and therefore tends to be under closer scrutiny) so there are obvious links with the pink components of the self-efficacy domain (see Chapter 11). Adrian knows that he is failing to meet the national requirements in his avoidance of teaching regular science lessons and, as a result, he is feeling considerable anxiety about the repercussions of this. He is keen to make a good impression and doesn't want his colleagues to find out about this weakness so he covers it up by telling 'white lies'. Adrian is disappointed with himself and is also worried about the consequences of being found out, especially as the head teacher has asked for a meeting to assess how things are going.

Another source of worry for Adrian is that, during the time that he was out of the country travelling, a major new national initiative aimed at raising and monitoring the achievement of students with learning difficulties was introduced into the primary curriculum. He has only limited knowledge of this and has still not accessed a copy of the document in order to familiarise himself with its contents. The initiative is frequently referred to during staff meetings and conversations between colleagues, but Adrian is reluctant to admit that he is 'out of the loop' in this respect. He is not sure what the implications are exactly for the three students in his class with special educational needs, but there is a parent consultation evening coming up in a few weeks' time and Adrian is secretly hoping that these parents won't attend.

All these anxieties are impacting on Adrian's overall effectiveness in the classroom.

---

**Knowledge of national requirements (delivery and assessment of the curriculum): self-reflection exercise**

Think about a recent national education initiative that required you to deliver, assess or monitor students' learning in a particular way. Did you read, absorb and understand the requirements at the first opportunity and become a source of knowledge for others? Did you ask a colleague to give you the 'gist' or the key points to enable you to get by without too much investment or effort? Did you go into denial for as long as possible because you couldn't face getting to grips with yet another new idea?

Is this type of response the one you tend to use in other situations? Does this suggest anything about your **receptiveness** (the willingness or readiness to receive new ideas, influences, suggestions or impressions) or **responsibility** (moving from a victim state to one in which personal control is regained)?

Consider the ways in which an underlying insecurity about what you have to teach and how you have to teach it might affect your general classroom management skills.

---

## Pedagogy

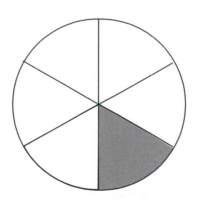

The focus of this 'blue' domain so far has been on knowledge about what is taught to students. This component is more concerned with knowledge about *how* teachers teach rather than *what* they teach. Pedagogy is defined here as the art and craft of teaching. This affects the range and type of methods teachers employ to impart knowledge and determines how they orchestrate learning in the classroom.

Adrian begins the lesson well by asking the students to reflect on what they already know about forces. However, the students are getting increasingly distracted by the presence of the interesting materials set out in each corner of the room and Adrian has to work hard to keep them focused on the task in hand. To relieve his growing sense of discomfort, Adrian quickly moves the students into the practical activity.

Although Adrian is aware of the importance of encouraging students to discover and investigate ideas independently, he is relying on this teaching approach as a means of masking his lack of subject knowledge. He has not made the objectives of the activity clear, nor has he thought about how he can best promote and support the students' independent learning. Similarly, he is using collaborative learning through group discussion as a means of introducing the lesson but again this is a cover for his own insecurities. His weak scientific knowledge, together with his poor understanding of pedagogy in relation to the teaching of science, limits the range of teaching and learning approaches he is using in this context. An understanding of the range of methodologies that constitute best practice in the teaching of science would give Adrian a much firmer foundation on which to build his experience and gain confidence in his practice.

Adrian's difficulties with science together with his inexperience as a teacher led him to make a number of fundamental errors in the delivery of this lesson. His expectations of this class of 7- to 8-year-olds were beyond their maturity level (the expectations would have been challenging for a secondary-phase class). To expect these 7- and 8-year-olds to be able to organise themselves into groups of four without the dynamics within any of these groups presenting the potential for serious behavioural problems was naïve. The plan for the lesson (or rather lack of it) gave these young students too much choice and required too great a degree of self-direction and self-discipline from them (considering their maturity). This led to a situation in which, in the face of insufficient direction from the teacher, the students filled the void with their own 'control' struggles: hence the power battles that resulted in the classroom scuffle.

With a better understanding of pedagogy (through experience as well as through study) Adrian would have realised that his lesson plan for this class needed to be tightly structured, with short, clearly focused, timed activities leading the students towards the understanding that was the objective of the lesson. As the students had not previously been taught how to manage their own learning and ways of relating in such an open investigative situation, they had no previous experience to draw upon and no learned structure as a point of reference. Without this experience, most of the students felt insecure in what was a completely new learning experience. Had they received prior coaching in how to manage their learning and social relationships in this sort of context, Adrian's methods might have been satisfactory.

---

**Pedagogy: self-reflection exercise**

Think about a situation when you were required to complete a task but were given insufficient information and guidance about how to do it successfully. How did this make you feel? What did you *do*?

Now reflect on your own teaching practice and choose a lesson that you recently delivered. What were the learning objectives? Why did you choose to teach the lesson in this way? Can you think of two or three alternative approaches that might have been even more effective in helping the students to achieve the objectives or understand the key concepts?

Critically evaluate the extent to which your planning and teaching really take account of the needs of different learners. How do you ensure that all learners are engaged and able to access all parts of the lesson? Identify one change you could make to enhance this aspect of your teaching.

---

## Legislation

Education is one of the most highly regulated sectors of public life, and there are massive amounts of statute and regulation which direct the educational process and put educators at risk of legal challenge (Gold *et al.*, 2005). All teachers need to be aware of the legal framework within which they work, although precise details will depend on what type of school it is and where the school is located, as there are local as well as individual variations in law, as defined by the teacher's job description.

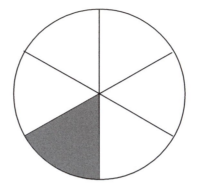

State-maintained schools in England face legislative prescription of a very high order, far greater than commercial organisations of comparable size and complexity (ibid.: 1). There is primary legislation (such as key Education Acts), but this tends not to go into fine detail. The detail is apparent in the regulations or secondary legislation, which the Secretary of State has the power to make. For example the detail of the National Curriculum, together with the rules relating to governing bodies or the method of carrying out special needs assessments, is all contained in regulations. Most of this detailed secondary legislation takes the form of statutory instruments. 'It is technically possible for the Secretary of State to specify not just what is taught in the classroom, but also how and when it is taught' (ibid.: 3).

Every teacher needs to be aware of both primary and secondary legislation and how it impacts on the educational context within which he/she works. To be ignorant of this context or to dismiss it as lacking relevance to the situation in which the individual is teaching can be dangerous for both the teacher and the students. Key areas where problems most frequently arise are special educational needs, disability discrimination, assessment, health and safety and child protection.

By avoiding the teaching of science, Adrian is failing in his duty, as a primary school teacher, to deliver a broad and balanced curriculum to every child. He should have ensured that he had an adequate knowledge and understanding of science and technology before beginning his primary teaching career. (This would have been taking full **responsibility** for both himself and those he would be educating.) Alternatively, he could have addressed the issue on taking up this first teaching post, by informing the head teacher about his specific weakness, indicating that support would be required. In not doing this, he is laying himself open to questions about his capability, but more seriously he is harming the scientific education of the young people he has been employed to teach.

It is also apparent that Adrian is failing to address the special educational needs of several students in his class. In failing to inform himself of the implications of the new national initiative and, more specifically, in not taking into consideration the social, emotional and behavioural needs of certain particularly vulnerable individuals in his class, Adrian is under-performing. The litigation and case law that surround provision for children with special needs are immense, and every teacher must therefore be mindful of the requirement to consider the specific needs of each student.

---

***Legislation: self-reflection exercise***

Write down what you believe the law states about your duties as a teacher in relation to the following:

- race equality;
- disability rights;
- child protection;
- health and safety;
- the use of sanctions (including physical restraint).

Make a point of checking the relevant legislation guidance to check that your understanding is current and accurate.

Are there any aspects of your practice that you need to develop or adapt to ensure that you fulfil your legal duties? How will you address this?

---

## Knowledge of school policies

School policies and procedures are often context-driven interpretations of the legal requirements and duties placed on schools as a result of the primary and secondary legislation discussed in the previous section. This includes policies relating to the curriculum and its assessment, student admissions, attendance, behaviour and exclusions, bullying, race equality, special educational needs, health and safety and staffing.

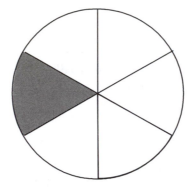

The responsibility for such policies lies with the leadership of the school (the head teacher and school governors). In most educational settings, responsibility for curriculum management is delegated to specific teachers or subject co-ordinators. Schools are required to follow regulations for both the delivery and the assessment of each aspect of the curriculum, resulting in each school having an internally agreed set of policies that determines all practice within the school. These individual school policies ensure that there is continuity and progression in the school's delivery of the curriculum. They also serve to ensure consistency in the teaching approaches adopted, which is essential if students are to build upon previous learning experiences.

In relation to behaviour, one of the duties of the head teacher is to determine measures designed to secure an acceptable standard of behaviour and to promote self-discipline, proper regard for authority and respect for others. In particular, these measures should aim to prevent bullying and racial harassment. Most effective school behaviour policies outline the school's beliefs, values and core principles in relation to behaviour and provide a framework for promoting positive behaviour. Behaviour policies also set out an agreed set of rewards and sanctions as well as clarifying particular responsibilities of staff members in relation to students' social, emotional and behavioural needs.

Unless there are effective induction procedures in place, teachers who are new to a school may be unaware of this context-specific knowledge at the outset of their placement or employment. Good practice suggests that all new members of staff (including supply or substitute teachers and visiting professionals) are given a context-specific handbook that contains key information about the school's key values and way of operating. However, it also requires a sensitised awareness and proactive determination to 'find out' on the part of the new employee.

---

***School policies: self-reflection exercise***

Think about when you first took up your current teaching appointment. What were the most helpful aspects of your own induction programme and why? Were there any details about policies or expectations that you were not fully informed about and which placed you or your students at a disadvantage?

How conversant are you with your school's behaviour policy? When was the last time that you read it?

How important is it for teachers within a school to have a consistent approach to the management of behaviour? What reasons do you have for your views on this?

---

## Knowledge of individual student needs

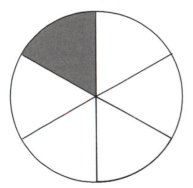

The final competency in the blue domain is concerned with specific knowledge (at the micro level) about individual students and their backgrounds, prior experiences, interests and areas of need. This micro knowledge helps to inform the teacher about where the student is in his/her acquisition of skills, and helps to identify barriers to future learning. Being sensitive to how individuals respond to stimuli and challenges and noticing and remembering patterns in these responses are important elements of successful teaching. Such knowledge informs the teacher about how each individual learns best (his/her preferred learning styles) and thus is powerful in helping to create the optimal learning environment for each student.

Within any class of students this is a massive amount of ever-changing information: ever-changing because of the characteristic 'flow' in terms of students' cognitive and emotional development. Learning styles can vary from subject to subject, and further changes occur as new skills, abilities and understanding are developed. To have this awareness of the overall pattern of learning within the classroom enables the teacher to be effective in directing additional support, helping individuals to overcome sudden blocks and providing additional challenge at just the right point. In this way the skilful and 'informed' teacher differentiates expectations and tasks, giving more meaningful student guidance, and thereby enables students to improve their individual performance.

'Micro' knowledge of individual needs also includes understanding the student's home culture (the values, expectations and challenges within the student's home environment as well as any potential barriers to his/her personal and educational development). Such knowledge helps teachers relate to and communicate more effectively with their students, as they are more likely to be aware of misconceptions or cultural barriers to understanding.

The scenario makes it clear that Adrian has had little induction both in terms of the school's policies and procedures and in helping him gain specific knowledge and understanding about the individual needs of his students. At such an early point in his teaching career he does not yet appear to grasp the vital importance of 'reading' his students to gain the essential micro knowledge to facilitate behaviour management and effective learning.

---

### Knowledge of individual student needs: self-reflection exercise

Think of a time when you attended a course or training event and the presenter assumed wrongly that all members of the audience were at the same starting point or had had the same prior experiences. Think about how you felt at that time and how this impacted on your behaviour as a learner.

How aware are you of the home cultures (home values, expectations, challenges or barriers to development) of the children you teach? Where do your perceptions and expectations come from? Is this a reliable source?

Think of a student whose behaviour you find difficult to manage and understand. Make a list of all the possible learning blocks he/she may be experiencing. What could you do to explore and overcome some of these possible barriers?

Think about the transition or transfer process operating in your school. How well informed do you consider yourself to be about the needs of each of the students coming into your class (or classes)? How much personal information about students (other than assessment data) do you communicate when they move out of your class?

## A review of Adrian – adopting a 'whole-brain' approach

If Adrian had developed the components within the blue domain, the initial scenario might have looked more like this:

It is Tuesday afternoon of Adrian's fourth week at the school. Adrian is planning his first science session with the class that he now considers to be his. It has been a strenuous, challenging, but very rewarding, three weeks of his new teaching career and Adrian knows that he has learned an immense amount about the 'craft' of teaching.

Three weeks ago, he felt very hesitant about his ability to teach science and technology. He knew that his understanding was relatively weak and his usual approach was to avoid facing up to those things that he felt less confident in tackling. However, after careful thought, he made the decision to go and talk to Maggie, the science co-ordinator, about his anxieties. Maggie was pleased that Adrian had sought her advice and spent well over an hour explaining the school's science scheme of work to him. She then took him through some ideas for lesson plans for the first half-term's study unit, taking the time to patiently explain the reasoning behind the different teaching and learning approaches. She offered to teach a demonstration lesson and gave him the name of an advisory teacher as a contact for further professional development. Adrian came away

from the meeting with increased confidence and understanding, some practical resources and a number of reference points
to follow up in his own time. A few days later, he asked Mike,
the technology co-ordinator, if he could have some advice in
the teaching of that subject too. During the course of this
helpful chat, Adrian felt able to confess that he had no real
knowledge of the new SEN initiative, owing to his travels
abroad, and Mike gave him a copy of the document to read.

As a result of this scaffolding approach Adrian discovered a
new-found determination to do the very best for the young
people in his class. Through hard work and some long hours,
Adrian can now see that he is delivering high-quality learning
experiences across the curriculum.

This sense of his own success as a teacher is exciting and
motivating, and is helping Adrian to renew his energy so that
he can keep going on what is a very sharp learning incline. His
greatest personal challenge has been to face his own initial
inadequacy and lack of enthusiasm for science. His determination to do something about this gap came out of his con-
science about negatively affecting the learning experiences of
the students in his class.

Adrian's increasing knowledge and understanding of the
curriculum that he is delivering, together with his sense of
being able to provide high-quality learning experiences, have
raised his confidence as a teacher. This enhanced self-belief (see
Chapter 11) together with his awareness that he is learning the
craft of teaching from his students every minute of every lesson
is enabling him to 'read' his classroom in a way that he was
unable to understand as a trainee teacher.

The result is a well-planned, carefully delivered curriculum,
tailored to meet the needs, interests and maturity levels of his
students in a highly structured learning environment in which
every individual feels understood and valued. The individual
student's social, emotional and behavioural needs are swiftly
recognised and issues are addressed within the context of the
teacher–student relationship.

*Table 7.1* Knowledge self-review

| What aspect of knowledge do I want to improve? | What can I do to improve this? | How will this impact on my management of behaviour? |
| --- | --- | --- |
|  |  |  |

# Grouping the grey

## Organisation

> Success depends upon previous preparation and without such preparation there is sure to be failure.
>
> (Confucius, 551–479 BC)

### The story of Hayley

Hayley is a young and enthusiastic modern foreign languages (MFL) teacher who has been working in the same secondary school for the past six years. She is a cheerful, outgoing and popular member of staff, always willing to volunteer although she frequently forgets to carry out the things she has promised! Hayley is an effective communicator and she has excellent rapport with her students. She is a gifted linguist and has strong subject knowledge but she has always

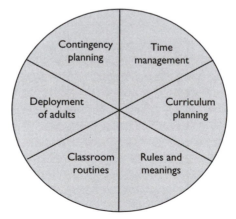

*Figure 8.1* Grey components.

experienced some difficulties in relation to student behaviour, owing to her lack of organisational skills. Read the description of a typical French lesson outlined below:

Hayley's class of Year 9 students (aged 13–14) have arrived for their French lesson and are making a lot of noise as they gather outside the classroom waiting for Hayley to arrive. She is frequently late for the beginning of lessons. The Spanish teacher (disturbed by all the noise) comes out of the room next door and tells the students to go into their classroom quietly and get themselves ready for the start of the lesson.

Hayley rushes into the room a few minutes later and, seeing them settling down ready to begin, she praises them for their sensible behaviour. She is out of breath, as she has been running from the staffroom after doing some last-minute photocopying of activity worksheets. As pre-arranged by Hayley, the language assistant is waiting in a study room down the corridor and is expecting to be sent a group of students for French conversation practice.

Hayley begins the lesson with the normal exchange of French salutations, after which she shares the learning intention for this lesson and explains how this will be achieved. Immediately, one of the students complains loudly, saying that last week Hayley had promised that today's lesson would be watching a French video. Other students confirm this and complain that Hayley is not keeping her word. She begins to feel flustered, remembering that this was indeed the case.

Hayley explains that the change of activity was an honest mistake on her part but that what she has planned for this lesson is equally enjoyable. In order to placate them and stop the growing dissent, Hayley quickly restructures her lesson plan and tells them she has a CD for them to listen to instead. The students continue to complain, demanding to know when they will see the promised video while Hayley rummages in her very disorganised cupboard for the CD in question.

Having located it, Hayley opens the CD case and realises with horror that it contains the wrong CD (Hayley's boyfriend constantly complains about this habit of hers). She is thrown by this situation and has the dawning realisation that she cannot afford to fall back on her usual strategy for covering her organisational inadequacy, which is to engage the class in conversation on teenage topics. The reason is that at the end of this session she has to feed back to her head of department about the learning that has been achieved and show student work as evidence, as this lesson had been jointly planned with him in order to help her meet targets set at her performance review meeting. She is very aware that questions are being asked, at management level, about the quality of her teaching and the progress of her students.

After some hesitation, Hayley decides that she must revert to the original order of the lesson, which is based on the reading of a French text with written answers to worksheet questions. Apologising again, she asks two students to give out the text and the worksheets. As this is happening she acknowledges the negative responses of many students but states that this work will help them in their forthcoming end-of-term assessments.

Hayley explains the task and gives the students good pointers for achieving a successful outcome. Within a couple of minutes of beginning the activity, one of the boys who had complained about the video pushes his worksheet off his desk and says loudly 'How do you expect me to do that?' Hayley immediately realises that she has forgotten to copy the differentiated version of the worksheet, vital for those students with greater support needs.

Hayley swiftly moves across the classroom to quietly reassure the boy that she will help him, at which point four other students loudly complain that they too need help. Hayley is becoming increasingly anxious about the rising tension in the room and notes that at least half the students are still off task. At this point, the language assistant opens the classroom door to find out why she has not been sent her conversation group, as planned.

## Questions to consider

- Which one of the four key tools (**receptivity, resolute optimism, responsibility** and **resilience**) does Hayley show the least signs of employing?
- List all the things that Hayley forgot to do in this scenario.
- What could she have done to help remember them all?

- What impact might Hayley's behaviour have on her colleagues and their workload?
- How would Hayley's students describe her?
- Why do you think Hayley is so disorganised and forgetful?
- What strategies could Hayley adopt to help improve her personal organisation?

Now read more about Hayley below.

## More about Hayley

Hayley, who is now 29 years old, did not intend entering the teaching profession on leaving university. With her love of languages and European culture she had always assumed (since childhood) that she would end up working somewhere in Europe either as a journalist or as a translator.

Her mother had formerly been a primary school teacher and has pursued her own career by becoming a local authority school's adviser. Hayley's two older brothers are both educationalists, one being a lecturer in a city university and the other an assistant head teacher in a large comprehensive school in Scotland. Hayley's father left the family and emigrated to Australia when she was 10 years old and she has only seen him four times since then, although they exchange occasional e-mails.

During her own primary and secondary education, Hayley had been an unusual student, evidently gifted as a communicator in both spoken and written language. Later, it became apparent that these talents extended to an ability to learn other languages easily. However, these gifts were countered by some difficulties in other areas of her learning and, in particular, with certain aspects of sequencing and ordering. Though not extreme, these difficulties did make for bumpy progress in mathematics, in which she required individual tuition to achieve a pass at GCSE (General Certificate of Secondary Education). Her difficulties with sequencing also appeared to impact on her ability to organise herself, although this was often attributed to 'laziness' on Hayley's part, by her family and teachers.

Hayley went to her local university because her family anticipated (and she agreed) that she would need considerable support. During her teenage years she had required lots of family help to manage even the simplest organisational tasks, mainly because she was so forgetful and disorganised. Her giftedness and love of languages enabled

Hayley to achieve well at university despite her difficulties with organisation. Her warmth, charm and outgoing personality meant that she could invariably get herself out of any problems that arose, and studying so close to home meant that her mother was always on hand to remind and organise her.

Hayley left university with a good degree but, despite her hopes and ambitions, she never quite got round to applying for those positions in Europe. Seeing this opportunity, Hayley's mother strongly suggested that she did a PGCE (Post-Graduate Certificate in Education) as an insurance for the future. She persuaded Hayley by saying that, if the right job in Europe did not materialise straight away, she could always fall back on teaching until it did.

Having applied and been accepted for the course, Hayley completed her PGCE qualification, and was quite surprised to find that she really enjoyed many aspects of the teaching experience. However, her intention to work abroad was as strong as ever and, rather than apply for a teaching post, she took a series of casual jobs in bars and factories as she planned and dreamed about her future career in Europe.

Once again, Hayley failed to put her plans into action and, after several months of watching her drift from one low-paid job to another, her mother noticed that the local secondary school was advertising for a teacher of French. She even downloaded the details and application form for Hayley and reminded her (several times) of the closing date. Hayley was successful in her application and interview and has remained in this post for almost six years.

Hayley requires micro-managing by her head of department in order for her to meet paperwork deadlines, and he frequently has to cover for her lack of organisational skills. Her colleagues see her as fun-loving and caring but so scatter-brained. She even arrived at school once in odd shoes! Hayley enjoys working with young people and is good at making relationships. The students like her but get fed up when she doesn't mark their work. They also know that they can easily distract her during lessons, and this sometimes leaves Hayley feeling that she has been manipulated into talking about French films, music or teenage social issues rather than focusing on the lesson objective.

Hayley is aware of her weaknesses but so far in life she has managed to come out of most situations unscathed. She is very honest and has a high level of emotional literacy. However, she is denying the selfishness inherent in her poor organisational skills and lack of preparedness, because she is not taking **responsibility** for the negative impact she is having on her students' progress. She usually gets by on the strength of her charm but occasionally people lose patience with her. She has recently had her first informal verbal warning, as her students' end-of-year assessment results highlighted issues about their general progress. This has also triggered a closer analysis of her working practice, particularly the planning, assessment, record keeping and target setting for individual students.

## What do we mean by organisation?

Good organisation is vital for effective behaviour management because it supplies the structure within which the teacher and pupil work. This structure provides the essential scaffolding to enable them to achieve success. It also provides the boundaries which define the acceptability of all behaviour (in its broadest sense).

At a whole-school level, organisation begins with the vision of what it is the school is trying to achieve and how the school defines 'success' and shapes its ethos, values and educational goals. Organisation also requires a clear route map to 'success' that identifies how the vision can be reached. It clarifies the goals, identifies the priorities, sets targets and establishes the structures and processes that will enable the targets and goals to be achieved. Organisation also ensures that evaluation systems are in place as health checks for these structures and systems, so that the school has a view of how well it is doing. Organisation is essential for effective behaviour management, but this only becomes fully apparent when we observe situations with organisational deficit such as a lack of structure and scaffolding, poor vision or direction, no clarity of purpose or alternatively diverse goals that are inconsistent or contradictory. These are all factors that can contribute towards a chaotic learning environment. A school lacking in effective organisation may have no unifying sense of purpose, and staff may feel confused about what they are striving to achieve in their educational practice. Without shared goals, there is greater opportunity for conflict and wasted effort. Clarity about values and expectations are generally the basis of a school's ethos and, as such, usually serve as the foundation for a whole-school behaviour policy.

On an individual level, teachers with poor organisational skills can convey (through their behaviour) mixed messages about goals, values and expectations, and this is potentially destabilising for everyone around them. For this reason, organisation is an essential element of effective behaviour management.

## Organisation and the 'whole-brain' model

The skills associated with effective organisation are contained within the components that make up the grey domain. The six components are:

- time management;
- curriculum planning;
- rules and meanings;
- classroom routines;
- deployment of adults;
- contingency planning.

The way that these components can affect behaviour management are examined below, with reference to Hayley's situation.

## Time management

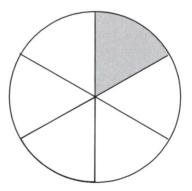

This component is an integral part of three other components within the organisation domain: classroom routines, curriculum planning and the deployment of other adults. Time management is about managing our most valuable resource, so that 'best use' is made of it, but this is determined by what the individual practitioner considers to be priorities. Time management within the classroom is fundamentally about values: values determined by the context within which the teacher works (including national, local and school-level requirements for education delivery) as well as those professional decisions the teacher makes about his/her own practice. For example, a teacher may decide to spend considerably more time or use 'optimum' learning periods (for example morning sessions) on those activities that he/she considers to be of greatest importance. Part of Hayley's problem is that she finds it hard to prioritise and say 'no'. Her natural affability and desire to please mean that she allows other people to move her away from her intentions. Despite her age, she is still unable to assert herself in her interactions with her mother and, although her communication skills are generally very good, she would benefit from looking at the component on assertive behaviour within the green domain (Chapter 9).

Time management is a key factor in behaviour management for a number of reasons. First, it enables the teacher to divide lessons into appropriate sections or periods to reflect the students' attention span. In this way, the teacher is better able to sustain student interest, with an adept teacher being able to carefully orchestrate the transition from one learning activity to another related task while keeping the students fully engrossed in the learning process. Such skills help to prevent boredom and frustration setting in (frequently the catalyst for unacceptable behaviour).

Another aspect of time management that can severely impact on student behaviour is the teacher's personal organisation. Being in the correct place, fully prepared and on time is essential for an effective start to a lesson or session. Arriving late has an immediate unsettling effect on the students. No matter what the students' age, a teacher's late arrival gives a poor message to students about their teacher's commitment to them. For some emotionally insecure students this can give rise to feelings of instability. The parameters provided by the structure of the school day no longer feel quite so secure, and this might give rise to 'boundary-testing' behaviour when the teacher does arrive. Careful time management on the part of the teacher helps the students to feel that the school is providing consistency and stability: factors that might be missing in a student's home situation. Hayley often arrives late for the start of her lessons because she has lost track of the time or because she is inadequately prepared and is rushing around trying to find teaching materials. This impacts not only on her students but also on her colleagues because they invariably have to leave their own classes in order to investigate the disturbance that is caused as a result.

Similarly, keeping to a set time structure within particular lessons helps to generate a consistent framework for the students to work within. This is particularly important for children and young people (such as those with Asperger syndrome, autistic spectrum disorder or emotional difficulties) who may otherwise experience high states of anxiety. Too often, Hayley allows herself to become distracted for long periods by the students' questions and then runs out of time in which to achieve her lesson objectives. The students have no sense of the lesson being wound up, and homework tasks are hurriedly explained without checking for understanding or time for clarification. This is unhelpful for all students but it particularly disadvantages any student with learning difficulties or attention deficit hyperactivity disorder (ADHD).

---

### Time management: self-reflection exercise

Do other people generally express surprise when you arrive somewhere in good time?

Do you feel guilty about letting people down because you don't get round to doing the things you promised them?

How often do you find yourself rushing to avoid being late for a pre-arranged appointment? How does this impact on your emotional state?

Reflecting on the way that you structure your lessons, how do you decide the amount of time allocated to each constituent part? What values are implicit in the way that you prioritise?

Do you often feel frustrated and annoyed with yourself because you feel you have wasted time? Think of some examples. How do you wish you had spent the time instead? What does this say about your own values and priorities?

---

## Curriculum planning

Time management also has links with this next competency. In the process of planning the curriculum, the amount of time allocated to each subject, each study unit within each subject, each lesson within each unit and each concept (key objective) within each lesson shapes the content of what is taught and learned and makes a statement about its relative value. If time allocation is carefully considered and well managed, the students are interested and enthusiastic about

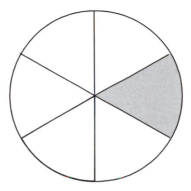

their learning so there is less scope for frustration, boredom and inappropriate behaviour.

Effective curriculum planning requires good subject knowledge; hence there are important links with the knowledge domain (see Chapter 7). An organised teacher will have a clear overview of how each lesson fits together to build the student's knowledge and understanding within a subject, and also what related skills and understanding are required for this learning to occur successfully. An example of this cross-disciplinary awareness is the recognition that in order to develop scientific investigation skills at primary school level the students require calculation and measurement skills. Having this overview of curriculum links enables the teacher to more easily identify gaps in a student's understanding, and this is important in minimising any frustration the student might otherwise experience.

Effective curriculum planning ensures that knowledge and understanding are built incrementally, at an appropriate pace (not too slow to allow boredom to take hold nor too fast so that the student feels swept away and the learning is not consolidated). Good planning enables the teacher to give students ownership of the learning process through the communication of learning intentions, individual targets and success criteria. Giving the students such ownership of their educational process can have a direct positive impact on student behaviour. Education is not something being done to them (which can lead to resistance) but a process over which they have some control which is seen as essentially beneficial.

High-quality curriculum planning also facilitates effective differentiation, which enables the teacher to meet individual students' learning needs, regardless of their prior attainment. Differentiation of learning materials can be time-consuming for the teacher but is essential for any diverse group of learners. If students are unable to access the curriculum, they will find other things to occupy their time and attention.

The teacher's ability to grasp the overall context of the learning (having an overview of how everything fits together) allows him/her to be responsive to student interest. Knowing the curriculum well and being able to see connections between key concepts or processes enable the teacher to make links between the new ideas being taught and those topics known to be of particular interest to the students. In this way, the effective teacher has more tools to engage the students and hold their attention.

> Any object not interesting in itself may become interesting through becoming associated with an object in which an interest already exists. The two associated objects grow, as it were, together: the interesting portion sheds its quality over the whole . . . An idea will infect another with its own emotional interest.
>
> (William James, 2005 [1899]: 46–47)

---

**Curriculum planning: self-reflection exercise**

How confident do you feel about your depth of understanding with regard to the curriculum that you are delivering?

How well do you know the wider curriculum framework that surrounds what you actually teach?

Can you think of a student whose 'difficult' behaviour may be related to his/her ability to access the curriculum? What modifications to your practice do you currently make to try to address this?

How aware are you of your students' particular interests (these may be related to age, maturity, culture, etc.)? Think of some examples of how you might use this awareness to develop an area of the curriculum that you teach.

---

## Rules and meanings

An important element of organisation within a school is defined by its rules. School rules tend to exist in layers. At one level, there are

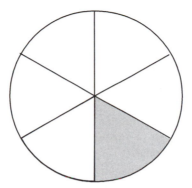

rules that reflect the school's broad ethos and fundamental values. Then, at another level, there are rules that relate to the school context (the physical features of the site, the number and age of students, etc.). These may include specific safety rules. For example, if the school is in a multi-storey building there may be a rule about always walking on the right-hand side of the staircase. The third level of rules is classroom specific and/or subject specific: rules that enable everyone to operate successfully and harmoniously in specific contexts. Rules at this level echo both the ethos and the safety levels. The balance of rules and rights in schools has been the subject of much philosophical debate for many decades but it is generally acknowledged that, when there is acceptance of and compliance to agreed rules, a school community can function more effectively and a greater amount of learning takes place than would otherwise be the case. The existence of rules minimises the need for long and drawn-out deliberations whenever disruptive behaviour needs to be addressed and provides a framework to help children and young people to develop self-discipline. Rules and their meaning are therefore an important part of the life of school.

As institutions, schools are concerned with education and learning but this is not limited to academic learning. Schools are also conduits for communicating behavioural expectations linked with social ethics and the concept of citizenship and thus are vehicles in shaping the culture and order of future society. The first layer or level of school rules is determined by the institution's view of what being a good citizen and good student entails. This is unsurprisingly similar in schools around the world. Definitions of good citizenship usually make reference to virtues such as moral development, personal responsibility, making a positive contribution to the community, taking care of the environment, maintaining social harmony and treating others with dignity and respect. Being a 'good student' requires giving and sustaining attention (listening, observing and concentrating), demonstrating commitment (being diligent, working hard and making a positive contribution to the life of the school) and respecting others (being kind, polite and considerate). These rules or behavioural agreements are frequently referred to as the 'golden rules' and appear in various formats with variations in wording but with a commonality of meaning which is echoed in the precepts of the world's major belief systems.

Students are much more likely to understand and adhere to school or classroom rules if:

- they are limited in number;
- they are straightforward and clear;
- the students have collaborated in the process of discussing and generating them in the first place and view them as reasonable and necessary;
- they are presented in positive and inclusive rather than prohibitive language (e.g. 'We raise our hand to ask a question' rather than 'Don't call out for help');
- the fundamental relationship between rights, responsibilities and rules is made explicit (e.g. 'We have the right to ask for help' and 'Other people have the right to speak without interruption': 'We raise our hand to ask a question');
- they are taught, modelled, displayed and referred to regularly.

Where behavioural expectations are made abundantly clear to students, and teachers are skilled in pre-empting unacceptable behaviour in the first place, it reduces the need for sanctions. However, for a rule to be meaningful there needs to be an appropriate and clearly understood consequence if it is not followed. To be most effective, a consequence should be carried out as soon as possible after the infringement has occurred and, except in the case of very serious and unexpected infractions, warnings (that allow students the opportunity to stop and modify their behaviour) should be issued before progressing to the consequence.

An appropriate consequence is one that is generally considered to be expected, fair, fitting and deserved; in other words, 'the punishment reflects the crime'. The underlying principle is one of reparation (making amends, repairing damage, restoring relation-ships and making up for lost time) rather than seeking revenge or teaching the student a lesson to make the teacher feel better! The restorative justice approach aims to improve behaviour in the longer term as it helps students to develop empathy so that they can begin to reflect upon and understand the effect of their behaviour on others (as well as on themselves).

An inappropriate consequence might be unexpected (no warning preceded it), unfair (applied generally to a group of students who were not involved), unfitting (making a student pick up litter for forgetting to bring sports kit) or undeserved (publicly humiliating a student). Inappropriate consequences such as these usually cause resentment, a sense of demoralisation and cynicism (Macgrath, 2000) and damage the teacher–student relationship.

---

### Rules and meanings: self-reflection exercise

How can you be sure that the students really understand what their classroom rules actually mean? How much ownership do you think your students have of the rules in your classroom? Were they fully involved in the formulation of the rules? Do the rules reflect the language that the students use?

How are the rules displayed? How frequently do you make them a point of reference with individuals or the whole class? Is this done in a negative context after a problem has occurred or in a positive context to help improve aspects of behaviour (such as listening skills) or to set targets?

Next think about the consequences (of rule breaking) that are applied in your classroom. What is the intention behind these consequences? Is it reparation or revenge?

Think of an occasion when a student reacted badly to the application of a sanction. From that student's perspective was the consequence expected, fair, fitting and deserved? If not, what might be the student's reasons for thinking this?

Can you think of any specific ways in which the consequences that you use encourage students to develop ownership of their behaviour?

## Classroom routines

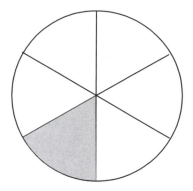

Human beings (and possibly all other living creatures) benefit from establishing and rehearsing specific routines or habits of behaviour to meet the set demands within individual contexts. The benefit of having such routines or habits lies in the conservation of energy that they afford: saving physical and/or cognitive and/or emotional energy. This is because, once organisational routines or behavioural habits are established, less conscious thought (as well as emotional energy if the behaviour has been a focus of some anxiety) is required to think through the performance of the activity, thereby preserving energy to expend in other ways. A well-known example of this lies in learning to drive a car. The learner driver expends a comparatively large amount of cognitive and emotional energy on the process of developing driving skills but, as these become established patterns of his/her behaviour, the level of energy required drops incrementally in line with skills becoming driving habits or established routines.

Within the classroom, the beneficial effects of established routines for both teacher and student have been recognised for a very long time. In 1899, during his series of lectures to students and teachers, William James spoke of the importance of establishing habit and routine in the classroom to provide a sense of order and with remarkable foresight linked the process of learning new skills and behaviours to the concept of neuroplasticity (see Chapters 2 and 3).

When learning routines are fully established, teachers do not have to expend as much time and energy on explaining their expectations because the students already know the ground rules. Although Hayley has difficulty in the area of personal organisation, she has enjoyed some success in teaching and applying a number of classroom routines. For example, in one of her classes, the students spend the first fifteen minutes of each Thursday's lesson on a fairly complex board game that involves them competing to be the fastest at learning their individual sets of French vocabulary. The rules of the game are the same each week but the vocabulary and outcomes change. The students initially had to learn the routines and rules of the game, but now their energy is focused on how quickly they can learn their vocabulary.

Routine also provides direct benefit for individuals who experience any degree of anxiety. At times of particular emotional or psychological stress it can help to perform those everyday tasks that are part of our habitual routine. In so doing, we seem to be subconsciously giving ourselves reassurance that normality can be regained and, because habitual behaviours bring about a sense of stability and consistency, the adherence to routines can help individuals to manage their anxiety.

Within the classroom, routine can serve the same function, and this is particularly important for the anxious teacher as well as the anxious student or the student experiencing considerable stress in his/her life. Familiar routines in the classroom and expected patterns of behaviour can provide that much-needed sense of consistency and stability. Unfortunately, Hayley's general lack of organisation sometimes results in a chaotic lesson structure, which deprives her students of the security of well-known routines and patterns of teacher behaviour.

However, in the same way that too many rules can become counter-productive, too many routines can be difficult for some students to remember and for the teacher to enforce. A highly structured regime may also interfere with the natural momentum of a lesson. It is better to propose and agree on a small number of basic routines that help to maintain a calm, cooperative, respectful and purposeful working environment for everyone. To be effective, these routines (as with rules) need to be taught explicitly from the outset and then reinforced on a regular basis through coaching and reminding. The establishment of routines in any classroom takes time and effort but is usually well worth the investment.

On a broader level, school-based routine provides structure and cohesion for the whole school community. For example, the routines for entering and leaving the building, taking registration or roll-call, the physical organisation of furniture and resources in a room, behaviour expectations for movement around the school, the pattern of school assembly and so on all help to create a sense of sameness and regularity. Consistency and stability are key features of successful support for young people with social, emotional and behavioural needs, but they are also of importance in ensuring the well-being of everyone. Consistency and stability are factors which help to reduce the arousal of extreme emotion, and a brain flooded with extreme emotion is unable to learn effectively.

---

### Classroom routines: self-awareness exercise

Identify a few of the routines you use to structure your learning environment. What are the benefits of these routines or patterns? Could any of these routines be improved upon?

Think about the times when behaviour is more difficult to manage. Could these circumstances be improved by introducing certain routines?

Reflect on what you do during the first two hours each weekday, during a normal working week. Can you identify any patterns or routines? Try to imagine what the start of your day would be like if each day someone else enforced a different sequence to these activities. Alternatively imagine waking up in a different place each day whilst still having the same duties and roles to fulfil.

---

## Deployment of adults

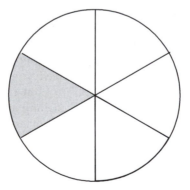

The most valuable resource in every school is human. Effective organisation means obtaining the best value from this resource, and this is the prime leadership and management task of every adult involved in education. An important organisational task for every teacher is ensuring each student fully benefits from the understanding, knowledge, skills, abilities and experience of all adults delivering and/or supporting learning in each lesson.

The teacher's curriculum planning, time management and classroom routines need to be such that every student benefits from as much direct adult input as possible. This input may be delivered in large groups, small groups or even individually, but it is essential that the student has experience of a meaningful exchange: a communication between the adult and student that imparts understanding, knowledge and skills; of equal importance is the adult's energy and enthusiasm for the subject. 'Elicit interest from within, by the warmth with which you care for the topic yourself' (James, 2005 [1899]: 55). Through such an exchange the student gains insight into the adult's thinking processes and depth of understanding. The direct experience of the adult modelling skills and understanding can be far more powerful and meaningful than learning delivered via secondary sources (visual and auditory recordings). It offers considerable opportunity for the student's interest to be awakened by this evidence of the adult's own love and enthusiasm for the subject.

Hayley evidently loves her subject and has the capacity to communicate this enthusiasm to her students, but her practice is hampered by her poor organisational skills. These poor organisational skills are also preventing Hayley's students from accessing the valuable opportunity and support that the language assistant's time could offer them.

Within most busy classrooms, effective deployment of adults depends on careful planning and good communication. The teacher needs to plan periods of time, specifying the exact form the support should take for every adult available within each lesson, which may include teaching assistants, behaviour support assistants and adult volunteers. The learning intention for the lesson will be the focus of adult support but 'the how' of achieving a successful outcome for each student needs to be specified by the teacher, as it is his/her responsibility to deploy adults in such a way as to ensure individual student needs are met.

It is essential that the teacher never assumes that supporting adults know the thinking behind the planning; this thinking needs to be explicitly stated. Effective support requires good two-way communication between the teacher and assistant. For example, the teacher might say: 'While I am explaining the task to the whole class I need you to sit with Sukraj's group and show them how they can use the bi-lingual dictionary to find the definitions.' Or the teaching assistant might offer: 'Once they have grasped that do you want me to support Harriet?'

When the teacher and the support adults communicate meaningfully about each lesson's learning intentions, individual student needs, the classroom strategies to be deployed, the adult roles and responsibilities within each lesson, and so on, it results in classroom organisation that supports learning in a well-ordered and calm environment.

When adult roles and responsibilities are clearly defined and expectations are shared, there is less opportunity for problems to escalate and for disturbances or grievances to arise and spread. Through careful preparation and training, supporting adults will be looking out for any early indicator of student frustration and taking appropriate diversionary action. Teaching assistants have ideally built relationships with their students over time and as a result will know a range of positive, refocusing strategies that are known to be effective with each individual.

Effective organisation requires effective deployment of all adults within each lesson. When this deployment is carefully considered, the learning gains for all students are immense. For the adults themselves there is greater satisfaction as a result of knowing good organisation is maximising the difference they are able to make in the learning and lives of the students. Hayley's language assistant would be feeling significant frustration that her important role in student learning was being sabotaged by a teacher's dismal organisation.

---

### Deployment of adults: self-reflection exercise

How much specific direction do you put into your lesson planning for your teaching assistants?

Are you fully utilising the knowledge, understanding, skills and abilities of these adults? Could you use their talents more creatively or to greater effect?

Do you share all your insights into the students' needs, interests and abilities with the supporting adults? Do you invite them to share their insights into the students with you?

How effective is your 'in-lesson' communication with your

assistants? Are you able to swiftly redirect support without interrupting the flow of teaching and learning or distracting students by having a lengthy discussion?

Do your teaching assistants fully comprehend the learning intentions you set and share the goals you have for individual students' learning and behaviour? If this is not the case, how could this be addressed?

## Contingency planning

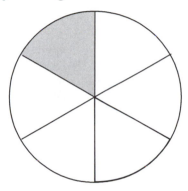

Contingency planning is about always expecting the unexpected and being prepared for it. It is asking the 'What if?' question and thinking through the course of action that could be taken in the worst-case scenario. This is not just an exercise that ensures that the teacher has 'safety net' lessons for when the classroom technology does not work or has assessed the risks and knows what steps to take if a student becomes violent during a lesson, but it serves to bolster the teacher's confidence in his/her ability to handle all that might happen. Contingency planning and having confidence in one's ability to handle whatever occurs (as a result of organisation and preparedness) is an important element of **resilience** which, in turn, helps individuals to sustain their **resolute optimism** and approach challenges with a positive frame of mind. Teachers who are positive and energised seem to generate a form of emotional elasticity that helps them to be more flexible and adaptable when facing problems. This aspect is covered more fully within the pink domain of self-efficacy (see Chapter 11).

In its simplest form, contingency planning is about assessing risk and having plans (to address the risks) in place. Obviously, teachers and other staff in school need to know all the inherent risks in their school environment as well as in all the activities that they plan to undertake. They must do everything in their power to minimise any risks. This is prescribed in health and safety law. This should be extended to meeting the needs of students with social, emotional and behavioural difficulties. Good provision for these young people is based on a thorough understanding of their individual backgrounds together with knowledge of what supports compliance and learning and what is a trigger to extreme emotional arousal and the consequent problems (see also Chapter 7 on knowledge).

Bill Rogers (1998) and others stress the value of having a discipline plan that is worked out by teachers in advance (either as a collaborative activity or on a personal level). An effective discipline plan is reached through a process of imaginative reflection and consideration of what might happen in the classroom and what the most appropriate way of dealing with it might be.

At one level, this might include a hierarchy of planned steps or actions that the teacher will take to correct student behaviour. These responses would be planned in such a way that they graduated from least to more intrusive interventions (Rogers, 1992, 1998). This forward planning can include things to say as well as things to do. As for more serious or unexpected incidents, such as a fight breaking out or a student refusing to leave the room as instructed, the teacher with a well-thought-out discipline plan should be more able to act rationally and put his/her plan into action rather than reacting emotionally. This is rather like planning an escape route in the event of a fire or learning first aid techniques that may one day save a life.

Hayley would consider herself to be good at contingency planning. In the classroom, she is highly resourceful and thinks quickly on her feet when things do not go in quite the way they should. Because she has good emotional literacy (Chapter 10) she is sensitive to the mood of the class and so she instinctively knows when to change the direction of her teaching or introduce a new activity to motivate the class, or that a student is upset and needs a different approach. Often this is successful because Hayley is a creative and empathic teacher. On other occasions, she relies upon her natural charm and charisma to gain the forgiveness of others when she lets them down through her lack of personal organisation. This is a strategy that has served her well thus far, but when she forgets to bring important coursework or marked assignments into her senior classes the students are understandably annoyed and her managers in school are beginning to see through this rather manipulative aspect of Hayley's behaviour. In the scenario described at the beginning of this chapter, Hayley's contingency plan (allowing the students to listen to the CD) was induced by her absent-mindedness (forgetting about the video) but then dashed by her lack of personal organisation (she had put the CD back in the wrong case).

---

### Contingency planning: self-reflection exercise

How do you react and cope in the classroom when things do not go according to your plan? Do you blame others? Do you become anxious and panic? Do you think on your feet and act spontaneously like Hayley?

Reflect on what you would do under the following circumstances:

- A student suddenly collapses in your lesson.
- You smell burning during a lesson.
- A fight suddenly breaks out between two students and others begin to join in.
- A student gets very angry with you and rushes towards you making a fist.
- You realise that you don't have quite enough books to go round and some students will have to share.
- A parent knocks on the window and beckons to his daughter.

---

## A review of Hayley – adopting a 'whole-brain' approach

If Hayley had developed the full range of competencies within the grey domain, the initial scenario might have looked more like this:

---

Hayley's class of Year 9 students (aged 13–14) have arrived for their French lesson expecting to have to wait on the corridor as usual, but they are surprised at the sight of Hayley ready at the classroom door, greeting them with French salutations.

On entering the classroom they are immediately aware of a very different approach to her lesson organisation; the classroom tables have been arranged in readiness for initial group work with all the required learning materials placed at the centre of each group's table, a TV and DVD player have been set up at the back of the room in preparation for the final fifteen minutes of the lesson, and Hayley has written an outline plan of the lesson structure (with learning intentions for each part) on the whiteboard giving the students a clear understanding of the expectations for this session.

The student response is a mixture of hushed surprise and puzzlement at this change and conjecture at what has brought about this transformation in their French teacher. A few comments such as 'She must be on her way out', 'It won't last' and 'She'll never be able to keep to the plan' are smilingly ignored by Hayley as she briskly settles them into their group seating ready for the first part of the lesson. Once everyone is in their seat, Hayley reads the names of the first group to be withdrawn by the language assistant. She reminds them of the learning intention for their session and gives them a precise time to return so that they are back in the classroom for the lesson's second activity.

As soon as they have left the classroom Hayley embarks on a swift explanation of the group work task, for which she has written bullet point reminders on the classroom flipchart. She goes on to explain that during this work she will be supporting Harry's group but that if any other group needs further help they can refer to a specific website where they will find a similar example. However, she suggests that this should only be a last resort, as they will learn more by trying to solve the task themselves.

Throughout the session Hayley keeps referring back to the overall lesson structure written on the whiteboard, reminding the students of the learning intention for each part of the lesson along with her expectations for their pace of work. Needless to say there is some resistance from the students to this new, very organised style of teaching from Hayley, but she dismisses their grumbles with good-natured humour, reminding them that it is in everyone's best interests that high-quality learning takes place. She also suggests that in a week or so they will all have got used to these new routines, finding them helpful and reassuring.

At the end of the lesson she does a quick evaluation by asking the students to indicate which of her approaches they prefer: the way she was teaching last week or her new organised style today. She asks them to fold their arms if they prefer her new style and not fold their arms if they prefer her old approach. She also gives them the option of leaving the room if they do not wish to participate in this evaluation.

Hayley is very surprised at the results of this evaluation. She had expected most students to leave the room rather than take part, but to her surprise only two left, with the majority decidedly showing their preference for her new organised style. This has certainly given Hayley a more profound reason to review her teaching style, as until now the impetus to improve her organisation was largely coming from leadership and management team pressure and the impending disciplinary action. As a result of this evident student preference Hayley is now in the process of a radical rethink of a number of her assumptions.

Table 8.1 Organisation self-review

| What aspect of organisation do I want to improve? | What can I do to improve this? | How will this impact on my management of behaviour? |
|---|---|---|
|  |  |  |

# Chapter 9

# Grouping the green

## Communication

> The map is not the territory.
>
> (Alfred Korzybski, 1879–1950)

### The story of Douglas

Douglas is in his early forties and is responsible for teaching a vehicle maintenance and repair vocational course at a college of further education. Most of Douglas's students are part-time and are aged between 14 and 17. Douglas has a great deal to offer the young people whom he teaches. He has expert knowledge and extensive experience in the motor industry and he is committed to passing his skills and knowledge on to the next generation of motor vehicle mechanics. However, Douglas is becoming increasingly frustrated by

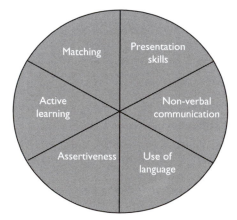

*Figure 9.1* Green components.

the behaviour and attitude that his students display, and this is draining his enthusiasm for teaching. To help understand why Douglas feels this way, read the following description of a typical workshop session:

For Douglas, Friday mornings are never easy. This is the time of the week when he has to teach a group of twelve disaffected 14- to 15-year-olds from the local secondary school. They have been attending the college every Friday for the past few months in order to sample a range of vocational courses. This is their fifth week with Douglas in the vehicle maintenance workshop. As Douglas arrives on the Friday morning, the students are already standing outside the workshop waiting for him to unlock the door. As he approaches, he notices that two of the students are smoking and others are not wearing their safety boots. This annoys Douglas because the rules are stated clearly in the student handbook that he gave them on the first induction session. He frowns and shakes his head but decides to say nothing at this point, as it will inevitably lead to arguments and he doesn't want to start off on a sour note.

Douglas unlocks the door and enters the workshop without greeting the students. The teaching assistant from the school, who accompanies the students to college, then ushers them in after Douglas and tells the two smokers to put their cigarettes out and come in. Douglas takes his usual seat in the corner of the workshop and picks up the register, looking round at the students as they enter and trying to remember their names. He can recall the names of the two female students but he realises that he can't identify any of the males. He makes a guess as one student walks past: 'You're Kane, aren't you?' The student is not Kane and he replies with an obscenity and the others laugh loudly. Douglas sees that some of the students have wandered over to the vehicles and are starting to open car doors. A couple of others are already selecting tools from the central supply even though they don't yet know which ones they will need. The teaching assistant attempts (unsuccessfully) to reason with the students and retrieve the tools from them. Douglas sighs and puts the register down before walking across to them.

He tries to get the students' attention but only about half of them appear to hear him. He announces that today they are going to remove and clean front brake pads and asks them all to 'Please come over to the chairs' so he can explain what they need to know. Two of the students comply and make their way slowly across the workshop; the others ignore Douglas's request. One of the students, Michael (who has only attended one session so far), says 'I don't need a lecture. I already know how to do that. I've done it loads of times', and he starts to slacken the wheel nuts and jack one of the cars up. Douglas hesitates. He remembers that this student was volatile and rude in the only session he attended – saying it was 'boring' and 'crap'. Michael sets about the task with confidence and Douglas can't help but feel impressed as he watches for a couple of minutes. He then hears the teaching assistant as she raises her voice in an attempt to keep order. Douglas praises Michael for his skills and adds 'But can you just leave that now for a few minutes and come over to the chairs while I explain to everyone what they need to do? They're getting silly.' Michael dismisses Douglas, saying 'You go and do your thing, mate, and I'll just carry on here.' Douglas is taken aback by this and wavers, not sure how to respond.

In the meantime, one student has gone back outside for another smoke, one is making a phone call and the others start to follow Michael's lead by jacking up the remaining five cars without permission. They have taken advantage of the situation because they find Douglas's verbal explanations so boring and long-winded. He talks in a monotone voice and uses words they don't understand. In previous sessions, he kept them sitting for almost an hour while he drew diagrams on the whiteboard and went on and on about safety regulations. All they wanted to do was start on the practical task.

Suddenly, a commotion breaks out. One of the students had been trying to remove the wheel but had forgotten to loosen the nuts before jacking the car up. Feeling humiliated, he had picked up a container of highly flammable cleaning fluid and sprayed it at the group of boys who were jeering and laughing at him. One of them grabbed the boy in a headlock and is now punching him for getting the liquid in his hair.

## Questions to consider

- How do you think Douglas would respond next? What do you imagine him saying and doing? What would the teaching assistant do?
- Identify and analyse the sequence of events that led up to this final outburst and general disorder. What were the key factors?
- Apart from communication problems, what other aspects of Douglas's practice might have contributed to the way that this lesson developed?
- Put yourself in the position of the teaching assistant from the secondary school. How would you describe Douglas? What emotions might you have experienced during this lesson and why?
- What words would Douglas use to describe this group of students? How would they describe him?
- What does Douglas try to communicate when he frowns and shakes his head outside the workshop? How would you have dealt with the smokers and those not wearing safety boots?
- How might Douglas have gained the attention of the group more effectively once they were inside the workshop?
- Why is Douglas taken aback by the way that Michael replies to him? How would you have reacted in Douglas's position?

Now discover more about Douglas by reading the section below.

## More about Douglas

Douglas grew up as an only child. His father was a successful engineer and, from an early age, Douglas would spend much time following his father around and watching him fixing things around the home. Douglas developed a keen interest in mechanics and technology and he would often choose to play alone with construction toys rather than engage in sporting activities or socialise with other children out of school. Douglas's father was pleased and proud that his son showed such aptitude in this area and, whenever Douglas asked how things worked, he was encouraged to go away and discover for himself.

When Douglas was 17, his father died suddenly after a short illness. As a result, Douglas changed his plan to study mechanical engineering at university and immediately left school in order to support himself and his mother financially. A good friend of his father's owned a local car repair business and was pleased to offer Douglas an apprenticeship. Douglas was a quick learner and an independent problem solver. He passed his professional exams with ease and at the age of 25 he was headhunted and appointed to a senior position with a much larger company, where he stayed for the next seventeen years.

Douglas never really got to know his work colleagues on a social level but they had great respect for his seemingly endless source of technical knowledge and he could always be relied upon to track down, diagnose and remedy complex mechanical faults. Douglas preferred to work on problems independently rather than collaboratively but was happy for colleagues to learn from him through observation. Six months ago, it was announced unexpectedly that the company was to close down owing to financial difficulties and Douglas found himself having to review his career. One of his colleagues had seen a newspaper advertisement for a college lecturer in vehicle maintenance and repair and he told Douglas that he should apply because he was 'so clever'. Douglas was flattered and, after careful reflection, agreed that it could be a great opportunity to pass on his skills and experience to the next generation of mechanics.

Douglas's perception of his students is that they have no passion for or even interest in the content of the course. He considers them to be lazy and lacking in basic key skills. He feels embarrassed by the obscene language that some of them use so freely and is shocked when they make glib references to car crime involvement. He had been expecting a much higher level of motivation and commitment but finds many of the students complacent and outwardly disaffected. During his demonstrations, the students fail to pay close attention and then are unable to follow the instructions for the tasks he has set them. Because of Douglas's upbringing and family circumstances, he is fiercely independent and expects others to take personal responsibility for their own learning.

There seems to be a repeating pattern to Douglas's teaching experience so far. Although the students are almost always initially enthused by the prospect of learning about vehicle maintenance, they quickly show signs of disaffection and their behaviour deteriorates after the first couple of sessions. As a condition of his appointment, Douglas will soon have to enrol on a part-time course of study leading to a teaching certificate and he is seriously beginning to question whether it is worth staying at the college and investing in training for a career that is not giving him the satisfaction he expected.

The responses that Douglas receives from his students are often unexpected and unsatisfactory. Douglas might conclude from this that he is not communicating very effectively. However, it is possible for Douglas to improve this situation and to become a more effective communicator by developing a more conscious awareness of his own patterns, habits and style. Through increased awareness of what constitutes effective communication when teaching and by developing and rehearsing the kind of skills outlined within this green domain of the 'whole-brain' behaviour management (WBBM) model, Douglas can become a more effective communicator and should experience fewer behaviour management difficulties as a result.

## What do we mean by communication?

Communication literally means making things common. The term itself is derived from the Latin word *communicare* meaning 'to share', but the sharing or exchange of information between human individuals is not as simple as it sounds. Whenever interpersonal communication takes place between people, a message is transmitted from the sender to the receiver in order to generate meaning. However, according to social psychologists, an estimated 40–60 per cent loss in meaning is likely to occur during this fleeting process. The way that we receive a message depends on our perception (and interpretation) of it and this may not be quite the same as what the sender intended, as every one of us experiences the world differently. The actual words that are used, the way they are said, the type of body language that accompanies the message, the ability and willingness of the receiver to listen to or otherwise 'read' the message, the presence of perceptual biases such as stereotyped assumptions, perceptions of power within the relationship, and individual or cultural differences can all distort intended messages and therefore create barriers to effective communication. The illustrative quote used at the beginning of this chapter, 'The map is not the territory', is there to remind us that multiple realities do exist. Our perception is just that – an individual perception – and every message has its own unique context. Since communication is based on perception, it is hardly surprising that our intended messages, including those that take place in the classroom, are not always received by others and vice versa.

## Communication and the 'whole-brain' model

In the WBBM model, communication is represented by the green components. There are close connections between this set of competencies and the lilac (emotional literacy) and pink (self-efficacy) domains (see Chapters 10 and 11). Effective communicators generally tend to be confident and sensitive individuals and, if there are identified shortcomings in one of these three domains, it may signal areas for development in one or both of the other two. This connection is further emphasised by the way that the three domains are grouped together within the wheel of competencies (see Chapter 5).

As with other domains, although the following 'green' components are presented within the model as separate units, there is a good deal of interconnectedness and overlap between them. The green domain comprises:

- presentation;
- non-verbal communication;
- use of language;
- assertive behaviour;
- active listening;
- matching.

These are now explained and analysed in turn with reference to Douglas.

## Presentation – transferring ideas and knowledge

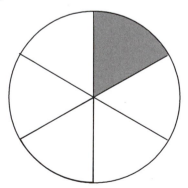

This component relates to presentational style and includes a range of skills that enable us to impart knowledge and other information in a clear, coherent and expressive way and to gain and sustain the attention of learners (or other receivers of our intended message). When thinking about improving our presentational skills or teaching style we need to consider what the learner sees as well as hears. We also need to be able to tailor our approach to meet the diverse needs of different learners. Effective communication involves making a connection between what we feel, think and do as well as what we actually say.

Social psychologists agree that non-verbal behaviour provides listeners with the most important clues about a message, followed by the sound of the message sender's voice. The actual content of the message (the words that are used) contributes the least amount (less than 10 per cent according to most studies). This has significant implications for the teacher. It doesn't mean that we can afford to give less attention to the content of our lessons, but we do need to pay attention to the whole package.

### Non-verbal messages

Because non-verbal behaviour is such a key aspect of communication, it is treated as a separate component (see 'Non-verbal communication', p. 136) and is only briefly discussed here. In terms of delivery style, however, non-verbal behaviour can play a very important role in enhancing or hindering the expression of ideas and concepts that we are aiming to teach. Posture and the way that a teacher stands and moves can convey confidence or insecurity, and gestures can be helpful or distracting to the learner. A moving object is usually more interesting than a static one, and this principle applies to teachers too! Those teachers who move around the classroom naturally rather than standing still in one place are more likely to sustain the attention of their students. However, it is important to be aware of unconscious pacing up and down, shifting weight from one foot to the other or other repetitive movements that will inevitably distract the students.

When addressing a group or class it is important to make eye contact with everyone as often as possible. Engaging with all students in this way can help to increase their attentiveness. Some presenters make a conscious effort to do this by mentally dividing the classroom or lecture room into sections and then deliberately shifting their gaze every few seconds from one section to another when they are speaking to the whole group. It is also important for teachers to 'scan' the room regularly throughout the lesson in order to monitor the behaviour of all the students. Kounin (1970) coined the term 'withitness' to describe this quality in effective teachers. It involves noticing, listening and pre-empting unwanted behaviour, even when your back is turned. When Douglas gets engrossed in the diagrams he draws on the whiteboard, he becomes hyper-focused on this task and has his back to the group for too long. Their voices are filtered out of Douglas's attention and he fails to realise that he has 'lost' them completely.

## Use of voice

When reflecting on the use of the voice and its quality, it can be helpful to think about tone, pitch, intonation, rate, clarity and volume. Being mindful of all these variables can help to maintain the interest of learners.

Voice tone (said to account for 38 per cent of a message) is more likely to be heard than the actual content of the message because it is associated with the speaker's attitude and affective state. Voice tone is the manner in which a message is articulated and, as well as emotion, it conveys social information such as mockery, arrogance or sarcasm. The way that Douglas speaks to the students reflects his general feeling of disappointment and frustration with them. There is no energy in Douglas's delivery, and from the students' perspective he sounds as though he is not interested in them as individuals or their learning experience.

Generally speaking, high-pitched voices sound less authoritative, less calm and less reassuring than deeper ones but they can be trained by pitching the voice down an octave (a strategy used by politicians). Intonation is about the rises and falls in speech, its rhythm and the emphasis that is placed on particular words. When Douglas introduces a task or tries to explain the working of a vehicle part, he hardly ever uses inflection in his voice and uses the same modulation throughout. Consequently, his delivery is rather flat and the students find his explanations boring. By including more questions in his teaching, Douglas would naturally use more intonation as well as engaging his students.

Good communicators use pace of delivery to maximum effect. When delivering important instructions or key learning points, effective communicators slow down their rate of delivery and use deliberate pauses to get their message across more emphatically. Very fast speakers not only make it difficult for listeners to follow them, but they tend to come across as nervous and unsure of themselves. Very slow speakers, on the other hand, may bore their listeners or engender feelings of frustration. Listeners may be tempted to try to complete the speaker's sentence for him/her or just switch off altogether! Enunciation is also vitally important for teachers. This is about speaking clearly and not mumbling, so that the students can understand every word you say.

Finally, volume is a key consideration. Varying the loudness or softness of the voice to suit the circumstance is a useful skill and it is worth remembering that a hushed tone can be more powerful in maintaining student attention than a raised voice. By varying the volume of his voice for different purposes, Douglas would be more likely to attract the attention of students when he needs to and keep his students interested during the instructional parts of his lessons. Shouting at a class is energy-draining and often self-defeating. It puts a strain on the teacher's vocal cords and, if it is allowed to become a habit, it sends out the message to students that raised voices are the norm. Because shouting is threatening behaviour it is also likely to evoke defensive patterns of behaviour from students, such as freeze and withdrawal or counter-attack. There will be times when it is necessary to raise the voice in order to gain attention but, for maximum effect, the volume should always be reduced after a tactical pause and once the attention has been obtained. Alternatively, the teacher could teach and use (age-appropriate) signals or cues for gaining the attention of the class, such as tapping a cup with a spoon, standing in a particular place, clapping, counting down from five to one, singing a song, or using hand movements that the children are required to copy.

## Content

Last but not least is the content of the message. An effective communicator is sensitive to the needs of the listener and understands that, for most people, attention begins to wane after only a few seconds of listening. Teachers need to be mindful therefore of the amount of information that students can absorb at a time and take account of this in their planning. Douglas tends to get so enthused in his explanations that he imparts more information than the students actually need or can use. He tends to use jargon and technical terms that are outside the students' experience and doesn't think to explain them. By always demonstrating the depth of his own knowledge, it could be that Douglas is satisfying his own needs here rather than thinking about the students'.

To keep the students more involved during his introduction to lessons, Douglas could ask more questions at strategic points and have an outline of the learning objectives displayed somewhere so that the students can see the purpose and direction of his explanations. This might also help Douglas to keep track of time and pace his lessons more effectively.

---

**Presentation: self-reflection exercise**

How effectively do you use eye contact when teaching a class? Try to become more aware of this aspect of your teaching. Make a conscious effort, when next delivering a lesson, to make eye contact with each and every learner (for 3 to 5 seconds) at regular intervals and make equal amounts of eye contact to different 'sections' of the classroom.

Have you ever considered watching yourself teach? This may sound like an uncomfortable prospect but, if you feel able, ask a trusted colleague to video you teaching a lesson. Watch it with the sound turned off and concentrate on your non-verbal behaviour. Do you notice any repetitive movements or nervous habits? Do you look comfortable and make good use of the teaching space?

Alternatively, you could make an audio recording of yourself to heighten your awareness of the language you use and the tone of your messages. Listen to the pitch of your voice. Does your voice sound tentative or authoritative?

---

## Non-verbal communication

Non-verbal behaviour generally operates at the unconscious level and is said to account for about 55 per cent of interpersonal communication. This includes posture, facial expression, eye contact, gesture, use of touch and use of physical space, all of which can accent or contradict the spoken words. Where there is contradiction (or

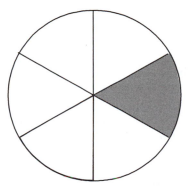

incongruence) between verbal and non-verbal communication this mismatch is highly likely to distort the message we want to get across.

The way that a teacher stands and moves can reveal a great deal about him/her. Standing tall (regardless of actual height) with shoulders and arms relaxed instantly gives the teacher an air of confidence and authority whereas a slumped posture suggests the opposite. Walking the walk as well as talking the talk is a behaviour that can be developed through conscious awareness, and even the simple act of walking purposefully around the classroom can make a teacher look (and feel) more confident. A well-known saying by William James is 'Act as if what you do makes a difference. It does.'

The amount of distance between the teacher and his/her students and perceived or actual barriers can have a significant impact on communication. Teachers who stay securely ensconced behind the 'barricade' of their desk automatically create a boundary that obstructs effective interpersonal contact and engenders a territorial feel to the room. The use of proximity, on the other hand, can be a powerful behaviour management tool. Firm reminders and warnings are best conducted privately and discreetly (it reduces embarrassment or threat to the student and minimises the spectator effect, both of which can fuel a challenge or counter-attack). Getting down to the student's eye level (and not towering over him/her in a threatening way) models consideration and invites the student to respond in an equally respectful way. However, unless the classroom is organised in such a way as to allow the teacher to access individual students, this will be problematic and the teacher may resort to making public reprimands.

Eye contact can be a very powerful tool in behaviour management. A stern or disapproving glare can often put a stop to unwanted behaviour without the need for a verbal rebuke. Similarly, tactical pauses can put a stop to low-level disruption and help to draw student attention back.

The intentional or inadvertent intrusion of personal space is uncomfortable for most people, and when this happens in the classroom it can often be the catalyst to angry outbursts. Personal territorial boundaries may be invisible but they tend to be fiercely protected from invasion by uninvited others. Unwanted intrusion includes behaviour such as looming or towering over other people, picking up or moving their personal belongings, sitting too close or perching on their desk, leaning in towards the face, and unwanted physical touching. The 'space invader' (who might be the teacher or a student) may be genuinely unaware of the effects of the behaviour on other people because he/she is simply not reading the responses accurately (see Chapter 10 for more about emotional literacy). Alternatively, it may be a deliberate strategy that is used to intimidate another person. Whatever the motive, this type of social behaviour sends out warning messages about power and can be perceived as threatening.

---

### Non-verbal communication: self-reflection exercise

Make a list of behaviours that might indicate boredom and lack of interest. Look for signs of these when you next teach a class. If you see them, make a point of injecting pace, altering your voice tone or changing direction in your teaching method.

What do you want your own non-verbal behaviour to convey in the classroom? Is there any aspect of your non-verbal behaviour that could be incongruent with this objective?

Identify one change at a time that you would like to make and try to be more consciously aware of that aspect over the next few days. For example, if you want to look more relaxed and confident, you could focus on adjusting your posture – the way that you stand, sit and move around the school. Later, you could think about what you do with your hands or concentrate on your facial expression.

---

# Use of language

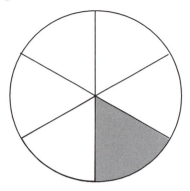

This component refers to the actual words that teachers use in their teaching and interactions with students.

## *Positive language*

Using positive language in the classroom has a number of advantages. It helps teachers to feel upbeat and optimistic and this can lift the general mood of the class. It also helps to prevent unwanted behaviour by keeping students focused on what is expected of them without the need to refer to the unwanted behaviour. It is the language of coaching, which is designed to motivate rather than demotivate learners. For example, Douglas might have used positive language to remind the students before they went into the workshop: 'Remember, you need to go straight to the seating area and be ready for registration.' Positive language is a core feature of assertive behaviour (see page 141).

## *Inclusive language*

Couching reminders and instructions in a way that includes everyone (including the teacher) can help to foster and reinforce an ethos of cooperation and cohesion. For example, a teacher might say 'What is our rule about that?', 'We need to finish this before break time' or 'We can't hear if two people are speaking at once.' Inclusive language should also be reflected in school and classroom rules or behaviour contracts (see Chapter 8 on organisation). Douglas might have improved this aspect of his communication skills by learning the names of his students. Making a point of remembering and using students' names is an inclusive behaviour that most successful teachers have to work hard at.

### Observational language

When Douglas noticed that two of the students were smoking near the workshop and that others had not brought the required safety attire he was unsure how to communicate his displeasure verbally. He wanted to avoid a confrontation at the outset of the lesson so he decided to say nothing at all, which conveyed a passive acceptance of the situation. Alternatively, he might have used what Rogers (1998: 68) calls 'observational language' as a way of demonstrating that he had noticed these infringements: 'I see that some of you are without your safety boots this morning, so when we get inside I'll explain again why you need to bring them each week' or 'I noticed that one or two people were smoking outside the workshop just now and I want to make it quite clear that this is not permitted for safety reasons.' Stating or describing the reality of the situation is less confrontational than asking pointless questions such as 'Why did you forget your boots?' or making provocative comments like 'Right, that's it! I'm confiscating those cigarettes!'

### Accessible language

Organising and presenting the lesson content using language that students can understand and follow is essential for preventative behaviour management. Learners do not always feel able or comfortable enough to admit that they don't understand a particular word or phrase but can quickly feel disenfranchised unless the teacher checks regularly that they are following and understanding the language being used. Effective teachers often rephrase important instructions in different ways and make a special point of explaining unfamiliar terms or jargon. Douglas doesn't think to explain what he means when he uses technical language or refers to specialist tools. When the students fail to carry out his instructions Douglas attributes this to their inability to listen.

**Use of language: self-reflection exercise**

Consider these teacher messages and reword them to make them positive:

- 'I don't want to hear anyone else talking when I'm talking!'
- 'No one is going anywhere until you stop this silly fussing!'
- 'I don't want any calling out of answers today.'
- 'Don't forget to bring your library book back tomorrow.'
- 'Try to finish this exercise without chatting to the person next to you.'
- 'Stop looking out of the window. There's nothing of interest to see out there!'
- 'Don't close your book! The lesson isn't over yet.'

Become more aware of the way that you correct behaviour. Try to avoid 'Why' questions, because they can rarely be answered to our satisfaction! By stating what you actually see or hear, you give the student less ammunition for arguing back. If the student does deny what you are saying, then repeat the statement decisively, e.g. 'I *heard* you using offensive language and it's not acceptable.'

## Assertive behaviour

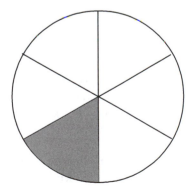

This component is about being able to express your feelings, opinions, ideas and needs in a clear, honest and open way that also respects the feelings, opinions, ideas and needs of other people. Respect (for both yourself and others) and a willingness to reach a compromise are central to the concept of assertiveness. Sometimes the term 'assertive' is used erroneously to describe someone who is pushy or loud or someone who likes to get his/her own way by making a scene. This type of behaviour is certainly not assertive if it leaves other people feeling humiliated, put down or intimidated in the process. Consider this in terms of teacher behaviour. The teacher who manages behaviour by using sarcasm, harsh words, threats or emotional blackmail may be perceived by some as an effective disciplinarian, but this approach can be damaging to children's emotional health and it is highly unlikely to foster effective learning. Assertive teachers almost always have complementary strengths in the lilac and pink domains (emotional literacy and self-efficacy – see Chapters 10 and 11).

In the scenario provided at the beginning of this chapter, Douglas uses unassertive behaviour in his interactions with the students. At the beginning of the lesson, he avoids making contact with them altogether and fails to follow up important rule infringements (some students have not brought their safety boots). This situation may have arisen because Douglas has not recognised the need to reinforce these expectations on a regular basis until they become established practice. This is explored further within the grey domain (organisation, Chapter 8). Similarly, there is no clearly understood system for allocating or collecting workshop tools, and students have quickly learned to claim the 'best' tools for themselves at the outset, before they even know which ones are required for the task ahead.

Instead of standing in the doorway and greeting the students individually as they enter the workshop, Douglas expects them to follow him across to the classroom area (for registration and the lesson briefing) but, again, this expectation has not been explicitly taught or reinforced. When the students fail to do so, he asks 'Can you please come over to the chairs?' The students who actually hear him receive this message as a weak request as opposed to a direction and, apart from two of them, they fail to comply.

Assertive communication is very important when giving corrective feedback or issuing a reprimand to students. It often helps to use 'I' statements such as 'I'm really disappointed that you have come here without your boots because it means that you will have to miss this session and return to school.' Note that the behaviour is referred to and not the person (as in 'You idiot! If you can't be bothered to bring your boots you can go back to school!').

---

**Assertive behaviour: self-reflection exercise**

Consider the following questions to ascertain your own level of assertiveness:

- Do you feel as though you are taken for granted at work?
- Do you ever pretend to make a start on a job that you want someone else to do and hope that he/she will notice and take over?
- Do you sometimes act as though you haven't noticed misbehaviour because you are not sure how to deal with it?
- Do you often make up excuses rather than tell colleagues that you'd rather not do something?
- Would you feel able to speak out and support someone in a staff meeting or case conference if you felt he/she was being unfairly treated?
- Do you ever tell a student (in anger) that he/she is stupid/pathetic/a waste of space?

(Adapted from Derrington and Groom, 2004)

---

## Active listening

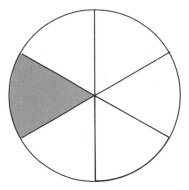

Active listening is not the same thing as hearing. The former is a skill that can be honed and developed whereas the latter is a passive sensory response. Goleman (2006) calls this communication skill 'attunement' and maintains that it can be achieved through motivation, a positive attitude and a conscious awareness or mindful state. It is an important aspect of emotional literacy (see Chapter 10) and an essential (but sometimes overlooked) interpersonal skill for effective teachers. The benefits of skilled listening include a heightened understanding of the students' perspective and enhanced relationships (both of which can help to improve the quality of teaching and learning).

Active listening has its roots in humanistic psychology and client-centred therapy and is about respect, acceptance and empathy. Key skills and qualities of active listening include:

- taking the speaker seriously (avoid pre-judging, discard prejudice and try to understand where the person is coming from);
- adopting supportive body language (lean slightly towards the speaker and maintain comfortable eye contact);
- concentrating attention (be aware of and dismiss distractions);
- asking open questions (allow the person to explain things in his/her own words);
- paraphrasing and reflecting (repeat the message you think you heard and check for accuracy and meaning);
- keeping quiet (avoid interrupting and allow silence – this gives the person the opportunity to elaborate, and it also allows those who are angry to run out of steam);
- thinking about what is being said (pick up non-verbal clues to read between the lines and consider the message from the speaker's frame of reference).

When Michael says to Douglas 'You go and do your thing, mate, and I'll just carry on here', Douglas is taken off guard and is not sure how to respond. He needs to check his initial interpretation of Michael's comment by saying something like 'It sounds to me as though you are refusing to follow my request, Michael.'

---

### Active listening: self-reflection exercise

When you are introduced to new people, do you usually remember their names and the details they gave you about themselves? If the answer is no, try to analyse why this is the case.

How does it make you feel when someone remembers your name?

Practise active listening. The next time a student tells you about a problem he/she has, asks for advice or wants to share some important news with you, make a point of:

- stopping what you are doing;
- paying close attention;
- trying to understand the student's frame of reference (where he/she is coming from);
- checking that you are receiving the message the student is trying to convey by using phrases like 'It sounds to me like . . . Is that correct?' or 'If I understand correctly . . . Is that what you mean?'

## Matching

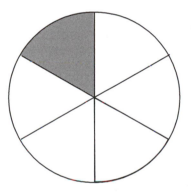

The process of matching or mirroring usually happens naturally in interpersonal transactions when two people have a natural connection with each other. For example, when talking with someone we like or get on well with, we may instinctively match that person's posture and body movements and adopt his/her style of language or type of humour. This is part of the process of building rapport and, although we may not be consciously aware of doing it, this type of matching behaviour ultimately helps us to feel more relaxed in one another's company.

Sometimes, however, this natural rapport is missing and communication is more difficult. In these situations, communication can be enhanced if we try to adjust our own communication patterns in order to achieve greater alignment. This process requires a heightened awareness of how one person's behaviour can affect another's during interactions between them. Matching is what happens when we speak slowly and quietly to someone who is angry and shouting at us. Our intention is to 'invite' the other person to match us in this way and lower his/her voice. Another example might be when someone talks very quickly at us. We either match the person's pace or deliberately slow down our own to encourage the person to calm down.

Although a moderate amount of difference can stimulate communication, we prefer to communicate with, and tend to be more influenced by, people who are not too dissimilar to ourselves (Rosengren, 2000). An understanding of the processes of communication through awareness of neurolinguistic programming (NLP) and transactional analysis (TA) can help us to develop greater self-awareness and minimise the differences and enhance the quality of communication as a result.

### Neurolinguistic programming

Neurolinguistic programming is a cognitive model of human behaviour and communication originally developed by Richard Bandler and John Grinder (1979). They began by studying the behaviour of successful people who were described by their peers as being influential and effective communicators. Bandler and Grinder suggested that most people have preferred or dominant receptors for processing incoming information (visual, auditory or kinaesthetic) but they discovered that the most effective communicators used all three and were able to shift from one representational system to another to mirror or match the communication style of the other person (Dimmick, 1995). This skill is a conscious attempt to 'talk the same language' as the person you are communicating with. For example, if a person has a tendency to use 'visual' language, they may say things like 'I see what you mean', 'I get the picture' or 'It looks to me as though you think this is my fault!' An auditory style of communicating might be identified by language such as 'That rings a bell' or 'Can I sound you out on something?' If you adapt your terminology to match that of the other person it is thought that this will enhance your connection with the person and enable better rapport.

## Transactional analysis

Transactional analysis (TA) is another model that is used to facilitate more effective communication. As outlined in Chapter 3, TA is a psychodynamic theory of personality and social interaction (with roots in Freudian theory and first proposed by Eric Berne). It is based on the premise that all individuals have the capacity to think and are able to decide their own destiny. In other words, no one can actually *make* us think, feel or do anything. We choose our own emotional responses. A key concept of TA is that of 'ego states', which are consistent patterns of feeling and experience directly related to a corresponding pattern of observable behaviour (Berne, 1961). The ego states are referred to as:

- Parent – feelings, thoughts and behaviours copied from parent figures in our lives;
- Adult – feelings, thoughts and behaviours that are direct responses to the 'here and now';
- Child – feelings, thoughts and behaviours that are replayed from our childhood.

These are nothing to do with our current age or position in life; they are the inner voices (see Chapter 11 on self-efficacy) that shape our responses to all kinds of stimuli. The parent ego state can be critical or nurturing, and the child ego state can be adaptive (compliant or submissive) or rebellious. Most people achieve a healthy balance of all three ego states in their daily interactions.

According to the theory of TA, whenever we interact (or transact) with another human individual, patterns of communication that relate to these ego states can be easily discerned. For example, a teacher may say to a student 'You're late again. Sit down!' This teacher is approaching the transaction from the position of critical parent, which will (according to Berne) immediately invite a response from the student's child state: 'Sorry, miss' (adaptive) or 'Why are you getting so stressed with me? I'm not the only one!' (rebellious). Alternatively, a teacher might say 'Would someone do me a really big favour and help me carry these to the car park, please?' (adaptive child) and receive the reply 'Here, miss. Let me help you' (nurturing parent). These are called complementary transactions, and there is a quality of predictability about them.

This rule of communication has particular significance for us as teachers, because if we 'invite' students in this way to respond to us from their child ego state, then we have to be prepared to deal with the 'rebellious' version as well as the adaptive one. If we approach transactions in the classroom from our adult ego state, we encourage adult responses back. For example, 'You've missed the introduction so you are going to need to borrow some notes at the end of the lesson in order to complete the homework task.' 'OK then. I'll ask Jennifer.' This type of interaction (adult–adult) avoids personal attack and encourages the student to take ownership of the problem (**responsibility**).

Crossed transactions occur when these communication rules are not followed for some reason and we don't receive the 'expected' response. For example, if a teacher said to a student 'You're late again. Sit down' and received the response 'I think you need to get yourself a new watch, miss. It's not even nine o'clock yet!', this would cause a jolt because the transaction has been 'crossed'. The critical parents have met! The likely outcome of such a scenario is that the person who has been 'crossed' (in this case the teacher) will move across to the ego state that he/she has been 'invited' into. The teacher might feel embarrassed, check her watch and ask one or two other people what they make the time (adaptive child) or say something like 'I don't care what time you make it – the lesson starts when I decide!' (rebellious child).

Douglas experienced a crossed transaction when he asked Michael to stop working on the car and come over to the classroom area. He intended to deliver his request from a nurturing parent ego state ('Can you just leave that now for a few minutes and come over to the chairs while I explain to everyone what they need to do?') but instead of getting the predicted child response of 'Yeah, OK then' or 'Do I have to?' Michael came back from adult saying 'You go and do your thing, mate, and I'll just carry on here.' This threw Douglas into confusion. Without realising it, he had invited Michael to move into the adult ego state when he added, rather conspiratorially, 'They're getting silly.'

### Matching: self-reflection exercise

Begin to observe more closely the way that people interact with one another. Notice the clues that reveal the quality of rapport. Look for the way that good friends match each other's non-verbal behaviour and move in synchronisation. Listen to the way that people tune into and adopt one another's preferred sensory modality.

Think of a student or colleague with whom you have a limited natural rapport and difficult conversations. What is it about your interaction with this person that makes you feel less than comfortable? Apply the principles of TA to help you understand why you might be feeling this way. Are you inviting their critical parent by coming across as child? Perhaps you are inviting their rebellious child by using critical parent yourself?

## A review of Douglas – adopting a 'whole-brain' approach

With improved communication skills, Douglas's lesson might have looked more like this:

It is Friday morning and Douglas's group of twelve disaffected 14- to 15-year-olds from the local secondary school have turned up for their fifth taster session in the vehicle maintenance workshop. As Douglas arrives, the students are already standing outside the workshop and joking with Sandra, the patient and good-humoured teaching assistant from their school. Douglas says 'Good morning, everyone' and then makes a point of checking that they are all wearing their safety boots this week. In the previous session, four students had turned up without them and had to be sent back to school because of health and safety regulations. He is pleased to note that all students have remembered this time and gives the thumbs-up sign to the four students concerned.

Douglas unlocks the door, holds it open and greets the students individually as they file past and make their way over to the chairs at the far end of the workshop. He compliments Kyle on his new haircut and thanks two of the students for remembering not to smoke near the workshop this week. He smiles at Sandra and asks her how the journey had been (she accompanies the students in the mini-bus). They share a quick joke and then Douglas takes the register, making a special effort to remember everyone's name.

Douglas begins the lesson by asking the students to recall what they had learned the previous week and then informs them that today they will be learning how to remove and clean brake pads. Michael tuts and says 'I know how to do that. I've done it loads of times.' Douglas replies by saying (enthusiastically) 'Excellent, Michael. Once you've shown me what you can do, I'll give you something more tricky to try. I know just the thing! But first, a quick look at the safety rules for today. Everyone looking this way then.' Douglas then draws the students' attention to the four key safety rules for this session that he had earlier written on the board. These are:

- Before you jack the vehicle up make sure that wheel nuts are loosened and ask Douglas or Sandra to check your jacking points.
- Use an axle stand to support the vehicle before removing wheels.
- Make sure you wear a face mask when removing disc pads (toxic dust).
- Ask Sandra to bring you the cleaning fluid when you are ready to clean the callipers.

Douglas explains why each of these rules is vitally important for safety reasons (and adds one or two graphic anecdotes that successfully grab their attention) and then gives the students a quick demonstration of how to remove the pads using a model calliper on the workbench. He invites two of the students to have a go themselves and then, satisfied that all students understand what to do, instructs one student from each working pair to collect the tools from Sandra, who is now waiting by the central store with her instructions. The remaining students are directed to wait by their allocated vehicles.

Douglas is pleased with the way the lesson has begun and relaxes visibly. Sandra feels that she is being useful at last and the students are relieved to be getting on with the practical task so early on in the lesson. Even Michael is looking forward to tackling the more challenging task ahead that Douglas describes to him as they walk over to the vehicles together. Altogether, this creates a positive atmosphere in the workshop.

*Table 9.1* Communication self-review

| What aspect of communication do I want to improve? | What can I do to improve this? | How will this impact on my management of behaviour? |
| --- | --- | --- |
| | | |

## Chapter 10

# Grouping the lilac

## Emotional literacy

> People may not remember what you did for them, or even what you said, but they will always remember how you made them feel.
>
> (Anonymous)

### The story of Sabia

Sabia is an experienced teacher and is head of the ICT department in a large inner city secondary school. She prides herself on her perceived ability to manage student behaviour. She demands respect from her students, insists on silence in her lessons and always expects students to comply with her instructions without question. However, Sabia has a reputation for losing her temper in class, and many of the students are fearful of her. In addition, her relationships

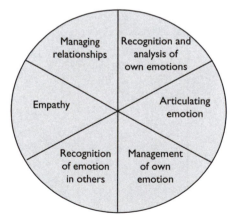

*Figure 10.1* Lilac components.

with colleagues are strained and those she line-manages feel unsupported and vulnerable, owing to her insensitivity and short temper. Let's discover more about Sabia by looking at a typical classroom scenario:

It is the final lesson on a Wednesday afternoon and Sabia feels obliged to cover a Year 11 class of 15- to 16-year-olds for an absent colleague. In three weeks' time, these students will be taking their final ICT exams. Sabia makes her apologies and leaves a senior management team meeting that has overrun and she arrives a few minutes late to cover the class. As she approaches the classroom, she can hear loud raucous laughter and the sound of furniture being moved. Sabia quickens her pace and feels her heart pounding and her jaw tightening as she prepares for the inevitable confrontation.

Poised for attack, Sabia throws open the door to see two boys straddling office chairs, racing one another along the length of the ICT suite and being cheered on loudly by their classmates. Sabia is furious and shouts at the top of her voice 'What the hell do you think you are playing at?' Her knuckles whiten as she grips her file more tightly and her face and neck become flushed. The classroom goes silent and all eyes are on Sabia, who is scanning the room intensely. Suddenly, the tension is broken by the sound of a muffled giggle, which triggers a similar response from a few other students.

Sabia cannot believe this lack of respect for her authority and feels outrage. She notices one student with her hand over her mouth and shrieks at her to leave the room. The student protests her innocence and points out that she was not the one racing on chairs.

Sabia slams her file down on the nearest surface and heads towards the girl. Through clenched teeth, Sabia orders her to leave the room. At this point Sabia is inches away from the girl and glaring into her eyes. The student slowly folds her arms and juts out her chin to murmurs of support from a few of her peers. She accuses Sabia of picking on her.

Sabia is breathing heavily now and feels her hard-won authority within the school is being totally undermined. She believes that she has to win in this situation at all costs to maintain her credibility as head of department. In her eyes this 'battle' has to be won and she has to be the victor. She is on the point of physically removing this student when the assistant head teacher walks into the ICT room and calls her name.

## Questions to consider

* Put yourself in the position of those Year 11 students. Why might you be tempted to behave in the way they did before Sabia's arrival?
* As a student in that class how would you feel as Sabia came into the room shouting?
* Why do you think some students giggled?
* Can you think of a time when you responded inappropriately under stress?
* What physiological signs made Sabia realise that she was becoming angry?
* Why do you think she became so angry so quickly?
* Why did Sabia assume that the female student had been one of the gigglers?
* Was the student justified in defending herself and in refusing to comply?
* At what point could Sabia have stopped this escalation without losing face?
* What might have happened had the assistant head teacher not arrived at that point?
* How do you think the assistant head teacher might resolve this situation?

Now read more about Sabia below.

## More about Sabia

Sabia is proud of her reputation as an authoritarian teacher. As already mentioned, she believes in strict discipline and expects to be obeyed at all times. This is the teaching style that she was exposed to as a child and her perception is 'It didn't do me any harm!' She sees no need to establish a warm relationship with her students, as she cannot conceive of any educational benefit from such relationships: 'I am here to teach and they are here to learn.' Because Sabia relies on an authoritarian teaching style, she lacks alternative strategies when she is challenged. On the few occasions in the past when students like the girl in the scenario above have been brave enough to challenge her authority, it has always resulted in a highly charged exchange that has required senior management intervention. Her perception of such student behaviour always generates a defensive and emotional response over which Sabia has little control. After one confrontation, a student accused her of physical assault, which resulted in a formal enquiry. Sabia knows that she can become very angry on occasions but she convinces herself that her anger is completely justified. Sabia fails to see the dynamic she brings into the classroom and does not see that her style and approach actually create the tensions that lead to hostile exchanges.

Although the school has a positive behaviour management policy, Sabia is resistant to this approach, believing that students respond better to her harsher and more punitive management style. She suspects that she frightens many students by her manner and language but this does not concern her. In fact she takes a pride in it. She has no comprehension that she is preventing some students from learning effectively because she makes them too anxious. She shows no real understanding or awareness of the impact of her style on the emotional well-being of the students.

Sabia considers herself to be a private person and prefers not to engage in staffroom chat. Although she has had a number of personal and health difficulties of late, she would never consider sharing this private information with her colleagues (she has recently separated from her partner and has also faced a cancer scare alone). Similarly, Sabia would consider it as a sign of personal and professional weakness if any other member of staff made any such disclosure or sought emotional support. Sabia was brought up to believe that it is an indication of strength and dignity to keep your problems to yourself. She was conditioned throughout her childhood not to cry when hurt or upset, and as a young child was admonished for boasting or showing off when expressing joy and excitement. Sabia's father was a perfectionist who taught her to work hard and achieve her potential. Sabia is close to her sisters but she has few friends and has focused all her energy on building up a successful career.

Sabia may be a highly motivated and dedicated teacher but she is lacking in emotional literacy and this creates a barrier to successful behaviour management.

## What do we mean by emotional literacy?

> To be emotionally literate is to be able to handle emotions in a
> way that improves your personal power, and improves the qual-
> ity of life for you, and equally important, the quality of life for
> the people around you.
>
> (Steiner, 2002)

The roots of emotional intelligence theory can be traced back to the
early IQ measurement movement. In 1920, Edward Thorndike identified 'social intelligence' as the ability to understand others and to
act wisely in human relationships. He maintained that social intelligence was different from academic ability and was a key element in
what made people successful in life. For the next fifty years or so, social
intelligence remained undefined and unmeasured, and psychology
was dominated largely by psychometric and behaviourist theorists
until Howard Gardner (1983) challenged the notion of intelligence
as a single and measurable entity determined at birth. He did this
through his influential model of multiple intelligence (MI). The
seven types of intelligence he identified include two varieties of
personal intelligence directly aligned with the affective domain:
interpersonal (understanding others) and intrapersonal (understanding oneself). Gardner's theory has had a significant impact in schools,
providing a theoretical foundation for recognising the different
abilities, talents and learning styles of students.

Two American psychologists, Peter Salovey and John Mayer, coined
the term 'emotional intelligence' in 1990, and proposed a hierarchy
of mental aptitudes and abilities. Salovey and Mayer argued that we
need to be able to recognise our emotions before we can use them to
facilitate thinking. Later comes the ability to distinguish between
similar groups of emotions (e.g. like and love) before achieving the
most sophisticated tier of being able to manage emotional responses
and being able to selectively engage in or detach from particular
emotions.

The concept of emotional intelligence was subsequently popular-
ised in 1996 by Daniel Goleman's best-seller *Emotional Intelligence:
Why It Can Matter More than IQ*. Goleman suggests that emotional
intelligence is more influential than conventional intelligence for personal, academic and professional success and he proposes a five-point
framework based on performance theory that comprises:

- self-awareness;
- self-regulation;
- motivation;
- empathy;
- social skills.

The term 'emotional literacy' is usually attributed to Claude Steiner (1981), a former student of Eric Berne, who developed transactional analysis theory. As a result of Berne's influence, Steiner's theory of emotional literacy is rooted in the concepts of stroke economy and ego states (as discussed in Chapter 3 and also in Chapter 9, which examines the green competencies in the domain of communication). Whereas Goleman uses the terms interchangeably, Steiner makes a clear distinction between emotional intelligence and emotional literacy (the latter term is perceived to be 'emotional intelligence with a heart'). According to Steiner, love (deep appreciation) is at the centre of emotional literacy. Although emotional literacy is often referred to as a single characteristic, Steiner identifies particular skills that can be learned and that can help to open up the heart and unleash love. These are:

- knowing your own feelings;
- speaking about your own emotions and what causes them;
- learning to manage your own emotions;
- being able to sense and tune into others' emotional states;
- having a heartfelt sense of empathy;
- knowing how to repair emotional damage (recognising mistakes, asking for forgiveness and making amends).

The term 'emotional literacy' is generally preferred to 'emotional intelligence' in educational circles because it reminds us that it can be learned and developed as opposed to being a fixed trait or innate quality. It is also perceived as affirming that we all have degrees of emotional literacy. Bocchino (1999) makes the distinction between emotional intelligence as a potential (or predisposition) that can be nurtured and developed in a person and emotional literacy as the constellation of skills and tools that we learn to become emotionally fluent. Similarly, Sharp (2001) describes emotional intelligence as a cluster of affective competencies and emotional literacy as the process by which we develop these. A key point that Sharp makes is that, before we can teach children about how to appropriately express and handle emotions, we as adults must learn how to do this ourselves. As adults we must endeavour to break some emotional habits that have become firmly established in the neurological networks of our brain.

Weare (2004) also acknowledges the importance of developing emotional literacy in teachers, staff and parents and identifies a cluster of competencies including self-understanding, managing emotions and making relationships, all of which contribute to what she calls 'social literacy' (ibid.: 2).

This theoretical overview illustrates how different typologies have been identified by various commentators. However, the four broad dimensions in Table 10.1 (adapted from Goleman's quadrant model) seem to be common throughout the existing literature on emotional intelligence/literacy.

## Emotional literacy and the 'whole-brain' model

In the 'whole-brain' behaviour management (WBBM) model this set of competencies is known as the lilac domain. The six components that make up the lilac domain are derived from this theoretical framework and are now explored in turn below, with reference to Sabia. The first three components relate to self-awareness and self-management and the latter three to social awareness and social management.

It is important to remember that, although the six components are all aspects of emotional literacy, it is possible for a person to be strong in some components and weaker in others. For example, some teachers may be able to regulate their own emotions effectively but be unable to identify emotions in others. In Sabia's case, she is aware of her growing sense of anger but is unable to regulate and control the actions that this emotion arouses.

Table 10.1 The four dimensions of emotional literacy

| Self-awareness | Self-management |
|---|---|
| Social awareness | Social management |

## Recognition and analysis of own emotions

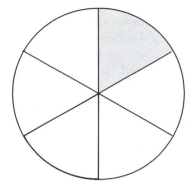

In its simplest form, this component is about self-awareness, being tuned into how you are feeling and knowing why you are feeling this way. Gardner (1983) referred to this as intrapersonal intelligence. Damasio (2003) makes a distinction between the observable manifestations of emotion (facial expressions, raised temperature, body posture, etc.) and the private feelings that are confined to the mind. This component therefore includes being aware of both the feelings you are experiencing internally and your physiological responses to them. Self-awareness is also about understanding your personal context and being able to recognise the triggers for your own spectrum of emotional responses from ecstasy through to despair. Impulse awareness or the recognition of personal triggers (irritants and stimulants), being able to judge your feeling state and knowing your own vulnerabilities are all essential prerequisites for being able to manage and regulate your responses.

Sabia was first aware of her rising anger as she approached the classroom because she felt her heart rate quicken and her jaw tighten. Other physical signs such as the gripping of the file and facial flushing were further indicators for Sabia. These are all natural reactions associated with anxiety and anger. Although she acknowledged these physiological responses, Sabia failed to take the steps to regain her composure at each stage and did not think through her choice of responses.

In order to avoid repeating this negative and unproductive pattern of behaviour, it is important for Sabia to be able to understand why she became so angry in that situation. Perhaps she was 'displacing' anger that had been aroused during a difficult management meeting immediately prior to the event or by her colleague's absence and subsequent need for cover. It could be related to fatigue and low energy levels at the end of the working day or it is possible that Sabia felt frustrated or anxious about missing the start of the lesson. From what we know about Sabia, she has a need to feel in control, and when she feels powerless her basic emotions take over. As Sabia hurried along the corridor, she was aware of being late and thus not in control of the learning environment when the students arrived. Whatever the reason for her feeling this way, it is likely that Sabia approached that class feeling less than positive. Putting the causes aside, the crucial factor was that Sabia unleashed this negative emotional dynamic which subsequently impacted on the learning opportunities of, and her relationship with, the students. Perhaps Sabia does not realise that the source of this raw emotion is her own insecurity.

Although Sabia was able to recognise her emotional state, owing to the familiar physiological responses, her analysis was incomplete as she had not been through a process of reflection and was demonstrating an external locus of control as she attributed the cause of her anger to the students and their 'immature behaviour'. Many teachers would have been irritated or disappointed by the students' behaviour in this situation, but Sabia's almost uncontrolled discharge of anger is both inappropriate and potentially dangerous.

### Recognition and analysis of your own emotions: self-reflection exercise

Do you see any aspects of Sabia's behaviour in your own? If this is the case how does this make you feel?

Do you know what irritates you about other people? (This includes colleagues as well as the children you work with.) Try to work out why they elicit these feelings in you. You cannot have control over another person's behaviour but you can control your own response to it.

Do you recognise any patterns to your emotional responses? Are there particular circumstances or contexts that always seem to evoke the same reaction from you? These could be positive or negative.

Are you able to gauge and distinguish your own emotional states? How do you know when you are angry as opposed to feeling mildly irritated, or pleased as opposed to feeling overjoyed?

What can you learn from your emotions? What are they trying to tell you? Try to complete this sentence: 'When I feel . . . I have an unmet need for. . . .'

## Articulating emotion

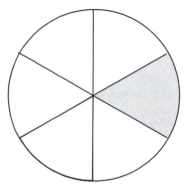

Building on this basic awareness of emotion and its physiological associations, this next component is concerned with refining the concepts through use of language. Many teachers will already be familiar with this component, as it is often a core feature of the emotional literacy curriculum, with its emphasis on developing an emotional vocabulary. It encourages children and young people to express and articulate how they feel. The theory behind this is that, without a specific language to describe emotion, children will be unable to conceptualise and differentiate their feelings. However, in order to teach and model this effectively we would argue that adults need to develop and refine this competency in themselves first.

We know that Sabia likes to keep herself to herself and that she was discouraged as a child from expressing her emotions openly. Her reluctance to share her thoughts and feelings with colleagues means that Sabia has no way of measuring or comparing her experiences or her reactions to them. Individuals moderate and regulate their behaviour by the reaction of those around them through a process of social learning. Since teaching is essentially a private activity (usually only one teacher in a classroom), this regulation will often occur informally through discussion with colleagues. This does not happen in Sabia's case because she actively avoids such interaction. Being able to speak about your emotions is not the same as communicating them. The latter happens largely at the unconscious level as people read and interpret our body language, facial expression, tone of voice and choice of language. The former requires a conscious willingness to disclose and share personal human experience and is an important part of the process of building mutual trust and developing lasting relationships.

Sabia is largely the product of her upbringing and it will not be easy for her to develop this competency. She was given the message early on in life that the expression of emotion represented personal weakness or a lack of dignity. When Sabia was a child, the significant adults in her life reprimanded her displays of emotion, so she continues to import and replay this script. The sight of students or colleagues having fun clearly displeases her and she has little time for those who complain about their misfortunes. This might help to explain her colleagues' perception of her as being unsupportive and may be the reason why she is reluctant to disclose how student behaviour makes her feel. Although Sabia may come across as a very strong and self-sufficient professional there is a certain fragility and brittleness about her that is preventing her from enjoying her career. Because of past events (parental complaints and a formal enquiry), Sabia has an increasing sense of her professional vulnerability.

Sabia would benefit from a frank and open discussion either with an objective coach or mentor or with a trusted friend or colleague who has considerable insight into the nature of her emotional literacy needs. This is the important first step that Sabia needs to take in order to develop her emotional vocabulary and build trust in the reactions of others. As Sabia's understanding of her own emotional responses increases, she needs to consider the relative strength of her emotions and ascribe an appropriate vocabulary which matches the intensity and range of her feelings.

---

### Articulating your emotions: self-reflection exercise

How comfortable do you feel about discussing your emotional state with others? Are there some emotions that are easy to share publicly and others that you would be reluctant to expose? Have you considered why this should be the case? (Shame, guilt, fear, disgust?)

Can you remember a time when you have offloaded a problem to someone you trust and felt energised as a result?

How comfortable do you feel when others choose to share their emotions with you? Is this a burden for you or do you consider it to be a privilege (to have been given this intimate insight)?

How skilled do you consider yourself to be in describing your emotions? Are you able to find the appropriate descriptors to communicate your feelings effectively or do you resort to clichés and non-verbal behaviour that can leave the other person confused?

## Management of own emotions

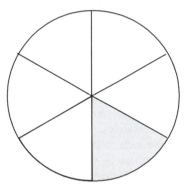

The competencies of being able to recognise and articulate how we are feeling are important components of emotional literacy, but without emotional management skills a person is unlikely to become emotionally literate. This is not to say that one should deny emotions or try to suppress them in some way, as this information is essential in helping us to make sense of the world and maintain homeostasis. But consider the example of a hypothetical colleague who is so tuned in to her own emotional state and so highly introspective and self-absorbed that she makes a habit of pouring her heart out to anyone who stops long enough to listen. Could this colleague be described as emotionally literate? Weare (2004) suggests that, unless emotional awareness is balanced out by other competencies such as resilience and emotional management, it can develop into 'paralysing self-centredness' and stagnation (ibid.: 32). 'Everyone feels all of the same emotions; it is what we do with them that makes us different' (Fisher and Sharp, 2004: 60).

This next lilac component is concerned therefore with the regulation and management of emotional responses. Essentially it is about taking personal responsibility for making healthy and appropriate emotional responses to the positives and negatives of day-to-day living. This involves both cognitive and behavioural processes affecting internal feeling states and external emotion-driven verbal and non-verbal responses. Emotional regulation and management enable you to keep a sense of perspective and allow access to a greater repertoire of responses.

Sabia does not manage her emotions very effectively. Years of suppressing how she is feeling have resulted in a denial of her own emotional states and the bottling up of tensions. This has had an adverse effect on her personal and professional relationships, and other people perceive her to be rather cold and unpredictable. Sabia is hardly the most popular or sociable member of staff. She regularly turns down social invitations from colleagues in an effort to preserve her professional image and discloses very little about her personal life. Because she tends to suppress feelings of frustration and resentment rather than deal with them, they eventually erupt as outrage and anger. Sabia doesn't consciously choose to become so emotionally aroused in these circumstances, but her brain literally becomes flooded with electrochemicals and stress hormones that prepare her for fight or flight. Goleman (1996) described this process as the hijacking of the amygdala, and once this state is reached it is almost impossible for Sabia to engage rationally. After these outbursts, she frequently feels low and depressed.

Sabia recognises the physiological cues that signal her impending anger but fails to act upon them. At this point, it would help if Sabia took greater **responsibility** and employed a strategy to break the cycle. This could be something as simple as counting to ten before opening the classroom door, consciously relaxing the body, breathing deeply, visualising a calm and tranquil place for a few moments, thinking through her response in advance and having a mental plan, or using positive self-talk or calming affirmations (see Chapter 11).

In the longer term, Sabia would benefit from learning anger management techniques. She might consider seeing a counsellor to help her understand the relationship between her displays of anger and her perceptions of threat. She could take up more exercise or engage in regular relaxation activities such as yoga or meditation and learn new ways of expressing her emotions creatively and assertively. Although Sabia may perceive herself to be an assertive person, this is not the case, as she relies habitually on aggression, intimidation and the abuse of personal power to express her wants and needs.

Finally, emotions are contagious (mirror neurons operate at a subliminal level) and the flow is likely to be top-down, so if Sabia is irritable, short-tempered and intolerant with her students and colleagues she will inevitably create a negative ripple effect (Kounin, 1970) and people will reflect these feelings back to her or on to others (Goleman, 2006). By shifting her perception of events and developing **resolute optimism** Sabia could be instrumental in establishing a more positive atmosphere where conflict and confrontation are less likely to occur.

---

*Managing your emotions: self-reflection exercise*

How do you usually deal with anger? Do you suppress it and bottle it up? Do you redirect it at someone else? What impact does this have on you and others?

How do you deal with fear and anxiety? Do you take to your bed rather than face the challenge? Do you turn to alcohol, nicotine or medication to help you through? Do such strategies solve the original problems in the longer term?

How do you deal with guilt? Do you find it difficult to apologise or take steps to make amends? Why is this? Is there always a valid reason for feeling guilty or are you being manipulated (or have you been) into feeling this way by the behaviour of others?

What does effective emotional management actually look like? Can you think of someone you admire because of the way that person conducted him/herself at a particularly difficult time?

---

Self-awareness is an important prerequisite for the remaining three lilac components: the recognition of other people's emotions, developing empathy and maintaining relationships.

## Recognition of emotions in others

Relationships would be a lot easier if people were completely honest in telling one another how they are feeling and what they are

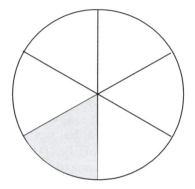

thinking. In reality, this happens very rarely so we are left to read between the lines, detect overtones or pick up visual cues from one another's facial expressions or body movements. However, not everyone is aware of how to decode non-verbal communication, and not everyone is emotionally expressive and therefore easy to 'read'. False reading of other people's emotions and the failure to detect incongruity between another person's emotions and his/her behaviour can result in mistaken action and reaction on our part. For example, we may react strongly to our misinterpretations and act defensively to perceived emotional threats that simply do not exist. These are sometimes referred to as 'false negatives'. For example, students may react angrily and aggressively to a peer who 'looked at me funny', or a teacher may feel outrage when a student refuses to make eye contact during a reprimand (owing to different cultural manifestations of respectful behaviour).

When Sabia hears muffled laughter, she reacts very angrily because she feels threatened and humiliated by this unexpected and 'inappropriate' response. Sabia expects the students to be submissive and even fearful of her, especially when she is reprimanding them, a response that she learned to adopt herself when her own parents and teachers were displeased. Sabia simply does not understand that anxiety and stress can trigger laughter as a nervous response. Since laughter is known to reduce certain neuroendocrine hormones associated with stress it is quite likely that the students giggled involuntarily as a means of relieving the stress that Sabia's (uncontrolled) behaviour induced.

When Sabia sees the female student with her hand over her mouth, she assumes that the girl is attempting to cover her laughter and is therefore guilty. A different teacher, with more insight into non-verbal communication, might have perceived this action of covering the mouth as one of surprise, fear or even embarrassment (the latter indicating empathy rather than insolence). Immediately after, when Sabia invades the female student's personal space and challenges her publicly, the student responds to this (her own) emotional threat by matching the hostile behaviour that is being directed at her. Anger is often preceded by fear. On both occasions, the emotional response of the student is triggered by Sabia's own behaviour. Recognising emotional responses in others can therefore be a way of helping us to develop greater self-awareness.

We know that emotions are bound up with learning and, if Sabia consistently fails to 'read' the emotional cues that her students send out, it is bound to have a significant effect not only on her relationship with them but on their responsiveness and readiness to learn in class (Mortiboys, 2005). Emotionally literate teachers are more inclined to 'tune in' and recognise the early signs of anger, anxiety or boredom in their daily interactions with students and, not surprisingly, teachers with a strong set of yellow competencies (see Chapter 6 on psychological application) are also more likely to be aware of these outward social signals as well as the more subtle and often unconscious expressions of emotional discomfort that are communicated or projected through words and actions.

---

### Recognising emotions in others: self-reflection exercise

People communicate on many levels. How aware are you of facial expressions, eye contact, posture, hand and feet movements, and body movement and placement?

If a person's words say one thing and his/her non-verbal communication says another, which do you pay more attention to? If it is the words, you may be missing the point.

When teaching, how do your students let you know that you have been talking long enough? That they don't understand? That they are becoming frustrated?

Read Chapter 9 (communication) for more on non-verbal communication.

## Developing empathy

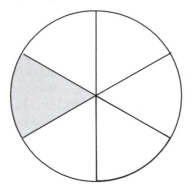

Being able to read or identify another person's emotional state and trying to understand its source is the first step towards developing the quality of empathy. Having empathy, however, is more than just recognising another person's emotions. It is also different from feeling pity for someone or showing them sympathy and kindness. Neither is it the same thing as emotional contagion, which is when people identify with strong emotions others are showing and become subject to the same emotions themselves.

The object of empathy is to connect with another person by gaining a deeper understanding of the person's predicament and responding appropriately. In other words, to show empathy requires us to give focused attention, convey acknowledgement and respond constructively and compassionately from a position of informed understanding of that person's frame of reference. It requires us to assume an alternative and non-evaluative perspective and involves the skills of active listening, non-judgemental reflection and the ability to communicate back to the person that his/her feelings have been heard, understood and accepted (see Chapter 9 on communication).

Because Sabia's own emotional needs are largely unmet, she tends to be controlling in her relationships and it is difficult for her to empathise with another person (view the situation from the other person's perspective). She is preoccupied with her own internalised insecurities and is therefore less able to develop empathy for others. Sabia protects her self-esteem in a number of observable ways: by reprimanding students in front of the whole class, by correcting or criticising her colleagues during team meetings, by keeping her distance socially and by denying and suppressing her true feelings.

Although Sabia is not naturally empathic or sensitive, there are steps that she can take to develop empathy, but it will require her to draw on her inner resources of **responsibility** and **receptiveness**. Sabia first needs to acknowledge that improving the quality of her relationships with her students and departmental colleagues is crucial if she is to help them achieve their potential. Her psychological need for control tends to create a climate of fear, and 'Fear makes people smaller – and less capable – than they really are' (Ryan and Oestreich, 1991: 46). Sabia models the authoritarian teaching style that she was exposed to as a child and, although she claims that it did her no harm, she may be denying her true feelings. Whenever we are belittled, rejected or ignored our basic emotional needs are invalidated.

As part of her self-reflection, she could 'try on' different roles to help her develop alternative perspectives (see the self-reflection exercise that follows), helping her relate to a wider group of individuals. Although Sabia takes an interest in the more diligent students who work hard in her lessons, she is unable to relate to many of the students she teaches. She may not be consciously aware that these students remind her of students from her own schooldays with whom she had little in common and to whom she therefore found it difficult to relate. She was quiet, obedient and hard-working, which is why she finds it easier to empathise with students who remind her of the young Sabia. In order to extend her empathy to *all* students, Sabia could make more of an effort to get to know them on a personal level. She could learn and use their names, watch them without judging, listen to what they have to say and show an interest in them as young people. She could consciously challenge the stereotyped notions she has constructed of 'others' by reflecting on their positive qualities rather than focusing only on behaviour that irritates her.

---

### How empathic are you? self-reflection exercise

Think of a teacher whom you liked when you were at school. Write down five words that would aptly describe him/her. Now do the same for a teacher whom you disliked.

How do you think your students see you? What words would they use to describe you? Be perfectly honest in your reflections. Are you happy with their description of you?

Think of a time when you have reprimanded a student in

public (i.e. in front of peers). Now imagine how you would feel if your manager reprimanded you in a similar way. How would you react?

Imagine yourself struggling to learn a new skill or trying to understand how something works. How are you likely to react if someone tells you to make more effort or 'just get on with it'?

## Managing relationships

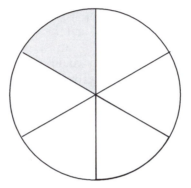

According to Goleman (1996) and others, the aspect of emotional literacy represented by this final lilac component (handling or managing relationships) is dependent on the mastery of the preceding components. Once individuals are in touch with their own emotions and are able to express and regulate them appropriately and have empathy with others, then they are well equipped to manage and maintain successful relationships. Given the difficulties that Sabia has in acknowledging her feelings and showing empathy, it is hardly surprising to discover that she is also quite isolated socially.

The effective management of relationships includes the ability to judge appropriate social, emotional and physical distance in verbal and non-verbal interactions with others, to know how to repair and restore damaged relationships and to be able to impact on and influence others in positive ways. This enables an individual to gain trust, motivate and inspire others and establish rapport with a wide range of people (and build group identity) as well as being able to de-escalate and resolve conflict. These are all essential key skills for effective teaching, and Sabia could therefore enhance her overall professional practice by working on this lilac domain. Greater competency in all these lilac components would also help Sabia to become a better communicator (see Chapter 9).

These are also important skills for Sabia as a team leader. Because of her commanding management style, she has generated a division between herself and her colleagues within the department. Rather than nurturing and bolstering their confidence, she is hypercritical and generally aloof. This has led to a dysfunctional, competitive and unproductive work environment. Sabia is loath to delegate tasks, partly because she does not trust her colleagues to achieve her own high standards but mainly to preserve her own perceived need for success and control.

People who are good at managing relationships also tend to be confident and positive individuals who feel good about themselves. Sabia's behaviour on the other hand has all the signs of a person with false high self-esteem. The way that she deals with situations is probably a reflection of how she really feels about herself. Her denigration of other people, aggressive emotions and need for control are all grounded in negative self-beliefs. Sabia would therefore benefit from working on developing the pink components (Chapter 11) to enhance her sense of self-efficacy.

---

### Managing relationships: self-reflection exercise

How comfortable are you when dealing with arguments between students? Do you manage to remain calm yourself? How often do you manage to resolve conflict to the satisfaction of all parties?

When you have a disagreement or falling out with someone, are you usually the first to apologise? Do you find it difficult to accept an apology? Do you bear grudges? Have you allowed a relationship with a former friend, colleague or family member to remain sour over a long period of time?

How comfortable do you feel about receiving a compliment? Are you able to say 'Thank you' and feel genuine gratitude or do you squirm with embarrassment or deflect the compliment in some way?

Remember a time when someone told you about his/her 'wonderful news'. How did you feel deep down? Genuinely thrilled for the person, a bit resentful or envious? Try to remember how you actually responded. Did your words and actions truly reflect your feelings?

## A review of Sabia – adopting a 'whole-brain' approach

Had Sabia developed these competencies within the lilac domain, the initial classroom scenario might have looked more like this:

It is the last period on a Wednesday afternoon and Sabia has offered to cover a Year 11 class of 15- to 16-year-olds for an absent colleague. She explains to her colleagues in the senior management team that she will need to leave the meeting in plenty of time for the start of the lesson but loses track of time and has to rush to the ICT suite. As she approaches the classroom she can hear loud raucous laughter and the sound of furniture being moved.

She quickens her pace and feels her heart pounding and her jaw tightening as she approaches the room. Recognising these signs Sabia takes a deep breath and slows her pace as she considers her options. She realises that the class have assumed that there will be no one to teach them and will therefore be taking advantage of this opportunity to have 'fun'. Sabia is disappointed that the students are not behaving more responsibly but realises that they have been under considerable pressure recently owing to their impending examination schedule and accepts that they have taken this opportunity to let off steam. Knowing she has a tendency to lose her temper Sabia relaxes her jaw, rolls her shoulders to release her physical tension and adopts a neutral facial expression. She clears her throat loudly and then opens the door slowly to see the students scurry to their workstations. She notices that two students have already logged on to their computers and are looking at their monitors. Sabia quietly thanks them for their responsible attitude and walks calmly to the front of the room. She decides to give the class take-up time and announces that the lesson will begin in two minutes by which time she expects everyone to have logged on and to be in the right frame of mind to start work.

The lesson proceeds well and before the students are dismissed Sabia thanks them for their attention and asks the students what the school's agreed procedure is when a class is left unsupervised for whatever reason. On being told the procedure by one of the students, she praises him for good recall but then expresses her disappointment that on this occasion the majority of the group had forgotten to follow this procedure. She acknowledges that they may well be feeling the pressure of their impending exams but reminds them of the importance of providing a good role model for younger students at all times and making the most use of every learning opportunity (do not waste valuable time). Her measured delivery of this reminder is effective in getting the message home. The students respond passively and some even apologise quietly as they leave the room.

*Table 10.2* Emotional literacy self-review

| What aspect of emotional literacy do I want to improve? | What can I do to improve this? | How will this impact on my management of behaviour? |
| --- | --- | --- |
|  |  |  |

# Chapter 11

# Grouping the pink

## Self-efficacy

> The greatest discovery of my generation is that man can alter his life simply by altering his attitude of mind.
>
> (William James, 1842–1910)

### The story of Trevor

Trevor has been teaching for ten years in a small rural primary school. He teaches a mixed-age class of 8- to 11-year-olds. Until recently, he thoroughly enjoyed his job and regularly received lots of positive feedback from pupils, colleagues and parents. Then, a year ago, a new head teacher was appointed following an unsuccessful inspection of the school. She has made many sweeping changes and, over the last few months, she has expressed dissatisfaction with some aspects of

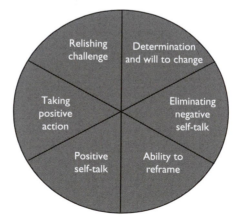

*Figure 11.1* Pink components.

Trevor's practice although she has not formalised this in a capability procedure. The result is that Trevor has begun to question his own ability to teach effectively, and this process of self-questioning and self-doubt has seriously undermined his confidence. Let's take a closer look at what is happening to Trevor:

Trevor arrives at school on Monday morning with a feeling of fear and anxiety in the pit of his stomach. He spent the best part of Sunday trying to plan his lessons for the week ahead but every lesson plan seemed unsatisfactory to him. The lessons seem dull, safe, and rigid in structure and he has even begun to doubt his ability to deliver the learning intentions effectively. He has no idea how to make the changes that the head has asked for and, in any case, he doesn't see much point in trying, as he feels that his efforts will be criticised. In short, he has totally demoralised himself during the course of his Sunday preparation. While he was planning, he kept hearing the new head's criticisms of his practice going through his head, and with every repetition of these comments he felt his energy and motivation flowing away from him.

On the previous Thursday, the head had spent the morning in Trevor's classroom observing him teach, examining his plans and evaluations and scrutinising the children's work. She had not fed back to Trevor until Friday afternoon. Although there had been a number of positive messages about his practice, the overall tenor of her message was critical, with key concerns raised about insufficient differentiation of teaching and learning in order to support and challenge every child. She referred to the 'zone of proximal learning', a concept that Trevor had not met before but he felt uneasy about admitting this to her. Trevor is largely unaware that the head teacher's demands on him are rooted in her perception of the task of bringing this school out of its 'failure' category. She believes that she can only do this by ensuring best practice from all staff. She also believes that, if individual staff fail to deliver, then they need to be developed professionally for the sake of the children's education.

On this particular Monday morning, Trevor's day ahead seems endless and full of pitfalls. His increasing self-doubt is eroding all the enjoyment of teaching he used to feel. The class

of twenty-three 8- to 11-year-olds (most of whom he has
taught for more than two years) is lively and difficult to manage, but this was certainly not the case six months ago. The
children appear to sense his failing self-confidence and are
asserting their views and demands. He feels as though they are
losing respect for his authority and gaining the upper hand.
There is more questioning of his judgement and, as his hesitation and self-doubt increase, the children's challenge of the
boundaries is also increasing. The children sense that Trevor's
firm rules and expectations are more negotiable. As a result of
this shift in power, the children's security and sense of safety
are threatened by the lack of teacher-set firm limits.

Trevor is acutely aware of the unacceptably high level of
noise in his classroom and moves across to shut the classroom
door. The head's office is just down the corridor and Trevor is
now sure that she is monitoring his practice closely. Trevor
speaks sharply to a group of children who are laughing together
at a nearby table.

## Questions to consider

- Put yourself in the position of the new head teacher. Why do you
  perceive Trevor in this way? Who influenced your thinking?
  (Inspectors, parents, governors, local authority?)
- Is the head justified in focusing her attention on Trevor's performance in this way?
- As a student in Trevor's class, what changes might you have
  noticed in his appearance, manner and behaviour over the last six
  months?
- What might be the physiological symptoms of Trevor's state of
  mind and lack of self-belief?
- Can you think of a time when you have been criticised or felt
  that you were being negatively judged? How did this impact on
  your performance?
- Can you think of a time when you doubted your ability to manage a class and teach effectively? Why did you feel this way?
  Where did the message that you were inadequate come from?
  How did you deal with this assumption? Did you challenge it or
  nurture it?
- How can Trevor's self-confidence be restored? If you were Trevor,

how might you go about this process of rebuilding your confidence?

Now read more about Trevor below.

## More about Trevor

Trevor had been an able student at university and completed his initial teacher training with relative ease, mainly because of his excellent communication skills and natural affinity with children, rather than his organisational ability. Both his parents were teachers and so Trevor grew up with good insight into the nature of the profession and its rewards and challenges. He had always wanted to teach and enjoyed the company of children and young people, and they in turn were drawn to his outgoing nature and sense of fun.

After graduating, Trevor was quickly appointed at this small village school located in an idyllic setting. The head teacher who appointed him had been at the school for a very long time, and Trevor soon began to realise that the teaching approaches and theories that he had learned about during his training and wanted to put into practice were being dismissed as 'new-fangled' and unnecessary. Trevor realised that, although the head teacher was well intentioned and dedicated to the children, he had low expectations of them and saw every externally driven educational change as an unwelcome imposition rather than an opportunity to improve educational practice.

Trevor's good communication skills and positive relationships with the head teacher, his two part-time colleagues and the local community led to him being able to bring about gradual change within the school through modelling good practice and enthusing his colleagues about better ways to deliver the curriculum. When the school was inspected four years after Trevor's appointment, the inspection team found the school to be satisfactory in most aspects and Trevor's practice was acknowledged as being very good. He was perceived as being a charismatic, able and enthusiastic teacher who was very much in tune with the children and empathic to their emotional needs.

Following this first inspection, Trevor's sense of self-satisfaction began to drift towards complacency and, having worked so hard at moving the school's thinking forward, he began to lose the momentum of his early years in teaching and gradually became infected by the inertia of his colleagues. He had always liked to work spontaneously, even at the expense of adequate planning and preparation, but he was beginning to rely more and more on this rather ad hoc approach. He became inward-looking and stopped seeking ideas to improve aspects of teaching and learning from research and professional development opportunities.

When the inspectors returned to the school for a second inspection a few years later, Trevor was shocked to find that the school was judged to be failing to provide an adequate standard of education and that his own teaching was deemed only to be 'just satisfactory'. As a result of these judgements, the long-standing head teacher immediately resigned, to be replaced by the new dynamic, troubleshooting, female head teacher.

Initially, Trevor could not comprehend how there could be such differences in the inspection judgements made from the first to the second inspections. It had thrown him into turmoil and his confusion lay in his perception of himself as an agent of change. He was shaken by the realisation that complacency had prevented him from moving forward at the same pace as educational change. He was now having to re-evaluate his self-image as a talented teacher (and a possible future head teacher), causing him to wonder whether he had been mistaken in his belief that he was a 'born teacher'. He felt his confidence ebbing away, even before meeting the new head teacher, and he found her suspicious scrutiny of his methods intimidating. Trevor was destabilised and became increasingly withdrawn and self-doubting.

At this point in his career, Trevor is lacking in self-efficacy and this is having a detrimental effect on his ability to manage behaviour effectively.

## What do we mean by self-efficacy?

The concept of self-efficacy is a relatively recent construct that grew unintentionally out of social cognition theory (Bandura, 1977). Social cognition theory is predicated on the belief that individuals are proactively engaged in their own development and can self-regulate what they think, feel and believe. In other words, they can consciously change and develop their cognitive functioning. The implication therefore is that self-efficacy or self-belief can also be controlled, changed or developed through a process of conscious awareness.

According to Bandura's theory, self-efficacy is the belief (or faith) that you have in your ability to achieve a goal. It is situation-specific, not a fixed trait, and is a major mediator of human motivation and behaviour. Although Bandura developed his theory of self-efficacy from studies of clinical syndromes, the concept was later extended to research in the field of career-related behaviours (Betz and Hackett, 1981). Since then, a number of studies have established that teachers with high self-efficacy show greater enthusiasm, patience and resilience (for example Ashton and Webb, 1986; Coladarci, 1992; Tschannen-Moran and Woolfolk Hoy, 2001). Bandura argued that strong self-efficacy beliefs are generally the product of time and multiple experiences, and Giallo and Little (2003) found that levels of self-efficacy generally improved during the first few years of a teaching career. Over the past few years, the notion of self-efficacy has also become the focus of numerous books within the 'self-improvement' or 'personal development' genre. This explosion reflects a growing and universal desire amongst a wide range of individuals for greater personal control in many aspects of their lives. This chapter recognises and makes reference to the contribution of this genre but is essentially grounded in traditional humanistic and cognitive behavioural branches of psychology as well as the emerging field of positive psychology (Seligman, 1998; see Chapter 3).

Bandura suggested that perceived self-efficacy comes from a variety of sources, such as previous experiences of accomplishment and failure (mastery experience), seeing other people who are similar to you achieve certain tasks or goals (vicarious learning), and verbal persuasion, encouragement or feedback from others (social persuasions). The latter source depends on the credibility, trustworthiness and expertise of the person providing the persuasion (Bandura, 1986).

People with high self-efficacy tend to approach difficult tasks with a greater sense of calmness and perceive them as challenges to be mastered rather than threats to be avoided. They also display an internal locus of control (Rotter, 1966) and are more likely to attribute failure to insufficient effort or deficient knowledge and skills, which can be acquired, rather than blame others or external factors. (This is an example of taking **responsibility** for one's experiences.)

High self-efficacy manifests itself as psychological well-being, including self-confidence and a healthy self-esteem. It enables individuals to have a reasonable, steady belief in their power to succeed and, as a result, engenders high levels of motivation, determination, energy and perseverance. This enables individuals to pursue their goals in spite of negative circumstances or the less-than-supportive reactions of others. A high degree of self-efficacy is also associated with the ability to bounce back after a major setback or life trauma.

Developing self-efficacy is not simple; achieving a firm, unshakeable degree of self-belief takes a considerable period of time (depending on the individual's baseline) and a great deal of mental work. Sustaining a high level of self-efficacy in the face of life's daily challenges means that the mental work has to be on-going. Self-efficacy is therefore linked closely with the key tool of **resilience**.

## Self-efficacy and the 'whole-brain' model

Within the 'whole-brain' behaviour management (WBBM) model, this domain comprises the set of pink components. These are:

- determination and will to change;
- eliminating negative self-talk;
- ability to reframe;
- positive self-talk;
- taking positive action;
- relishing challenge as an opportunity for growth.

This pink domain differs slightly from the others in the wheel because of the cyclical nature of the component parts. Self-efficacy is energising, which leads to greater effort and persistence. This in turn results in a better performance (a new mastery experience), which further enhances self-efficacy. The reverse is also true. Low self-efficacy is de-energising, which lowers motivation and effort. This often results in unsatisfactory teaching experiences, which further deplete self-efficacy.

It is also important to remember that most people have an imbalance in the development of these components. For example some teachers may have a high level of determination to develop and grow as practitioners but their ability to sustain their self-confidence through positive self-talk may be weak.

## Determination and will to change

Determination and will to change is based on an innate human need to 'grow', transform and generally improve our state or situation

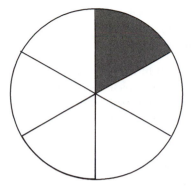

(sometimes referred to as the 'actualising tendency'). It is the element of self-efficacy that prevents us from becoming complacent and is the opposite of stasis, in which the individual denies the need for growth and change, preferring to work within known parameters, safe options and the status quo. The danger with stasis is the resulting rigidity of thought and action, with the individual stagnating and becoming too inflexible to adjust to the increasing and varying demands of life's flow and change. There are obvious links here with our key tool of **receptivity**, which requires openness to new ways of being and thinking in order to grow.

In the scenario outlined at the beginning of this chapter, Trevor's low energy and increasing pessimism about his abilities as a teacher are negatively impacting on his determination and will to change. At the start of his teaching career, his determination and will to change were strong; he continually sought ways of improving his practice as an educator in order to do the best for the young people in his care. He also wanted to help his colleagues to achieve the best educational outcomes, sensing that he could positively influence the educational achievements of the whole school. Trevor's self-efficacy grew as he received regular positive feedback (social persuasions) from his colleagues, school governors and parents. However, his increasing complacency over recent years and the changes that followed the last inspection have depleted Trevor's energy levels and, consequently, his ability to initiate positive action. He now perceives challenge as something that provokes fear and self-doubt. Trevor's anxiety about the behaviour of the class and his ability to retain authority has made him a much less creative and fun-loving teacher than he once was.

*Determination and will to change:*
*self-reflection exercise*

Think of an occasion in the past when you have made a determined effort to change an aspect of your life. What was it that gave you the motivation to change? (Mastery experience, vicarious learning, social persuasion?) Did you succeed in your efforts? Explore why you did or did not achieve your goal.

How strong is your determination to improve your behaviour management skills? Are there any recommended approaches or strategies that you are unwilling to try? Analyse the reasons for your reluctance.

Following a challenging lesson or professional meeting, are you able to reflect on what element or expectations you yourself brought to this situation? Did they play a role in the difficulties that you experienced?

Try to identify an aspect of your behaviour or thinking that is preventing you from being the teacher that you want to be. How strong is your desire to do something about it? What action will you take to address it? How will you maintain this determination in the face of daily challenges?

## Eliminating negative self-talk

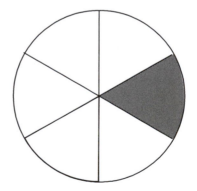

To increase self-efficacy it is necessary to firstly recognise the character and tone of what is commonly referred to as self-talk. This is the inner dialogue or internal voice that goes on inside your head and runs a commentary on your life's events, thoughts and actions. It is essential to realise the profound influence this voice can have on your energy levels and confidence; the first step is to be consciously aware of it. When Trevor was trying to plan for the week ahead, he was being constantly distracted by negative self-talk, which eventually convinced him that he was incapable of planning and delivering effective lessons. Every idea that he came up with was immediately quashed by his inner voice as Trevor continually replayed and distorted selected extracts of the head teacher's feedback. With his energy depleted Trevor lost his sense of **resolute optimism** and eventually stopped looking for creative solutions and gave in to his sense of inevitable failure.

Combating negative self-talk begins with awareness of its source and the realisation that you may have been self-programming over a period of time. Negative self-talk is bred from messages (actual or perceived) that are communicated by 'significant others'. In Trevor's case, he has been dwelling on the inspector's unexpected judgement for just over a year and now he has a new and equally damaging script to play since his meeting with the head. But such negative messages or 'life-scripts' are frequently the result of early childhood experiences. Transactional analysts such as Claude Steiner and Eric Berne refer to ego states, one of which is the 'critical (or controlling) parent'. Trevor was brought up with a nurturing style of parenting which encouraged his 'free' or 'creative' child. He is unused to dealing with criticism and it creates cognitive dissonance for him when the inspector and head teacher give their feedback. (See Chapter 3 for more about the theory of transactional analysis.) Whatever the source, this negative self-talk is life limiting in that it creates a barrier to growing and developing in a creative, confident and successful way.

To minimise the effects of negative self-talk, it is essential to have full awareness of the power of these internal messages or recorded loops (Seligman, 1998). Questions need to be raised about how these messages actually affect your emotional state. (For example if you were to say such things aloud to another person, how would it make him/her feel? What impact are such statements and observations having on your own emotional health?) Bringing the power of such negative messages into your conscious awareness enables you to realise the impact of this negative self-talk on your own self-efficacy.

The final stage in eradicating negative self-talk is to realise that you are in control of your thinking and that you are not at the mercy of the internal voice. It is possible for individuals to change the habits or patterns that have dominated their internal monologue, but as a rule people need some help in coming to this realisation and this is where coaches or counsellors can play a role. Eliminating negative self-talk requires constant vigilance against invading waves of negative messages about the self. As most self-talk has a habitual quality, it requires negative patterns to be replaced by new, powerful, positive patterns of thinking about the self. This change in the way that the individual thinks is essential in order to increase self-efficacy and confidence, which in turn impact on the individual's performance and relationships in the classroom. Changing to positive self-talk is believed to have an impact on human neurochemistry, flooding the nervous system with 'feel-good' chemicals such as serotonin and the body's natural opiates.

In Trevor's case, he is not aware of his own negative self-talk and therefore is taking no action to eliminate this negative inner monologue. His lack of awareness is resulting in diminishing energy levels and increasing pessimism about his abilities as a teacher. Trevor's current low self-esteem is draining him of the energy to initiate positive action and is creating a depressed state, in which all challenges appear to Trevor as insurmountable obstacles.

---

### *Eliminating negative self-talk: self-reflection exercise*

Make a conscious effort to listen carefully to your inner monologue over the next few days. Identify the times when the monologue is critical or questioning of your words and actions.

Make a note of the negative internal messages that you hear. Try to identify the source of these messages.

Think about a situation when you lacked confidence; try to recall the inner monologue – those cognitive distortions that were being played in your head. Are you able to see how you were conducting self-sabotage by the power of your thoughts?

---

## Ability to reframe

This component represents a central theme of the 'whole-brain' approach as it is concerned with perception, attribution and flexibility of thought. Reframing is also closely allied with the essential tool

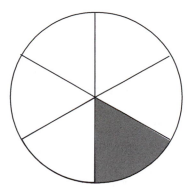

of **receptivity** in that it requires openness to alternative perspectives and ways of doing things. Reframing has its origins in communication theory and family therapy. It also features in neurolinguistic programming (NLP). 'By changing the frame through which we perceive an event we change its meaning' (Bandler and Grinder, 1981: 1). Within the domain of self-efficacy, the ability to reframe refers to the process of critically reviewing our perspectives in order to help eliminate negative self-talk and find new solutions to old or recurring problems. The specific problem may require a completely innovative approach, pushing us to reconstruct our views on how things should work or should be done. In changing our perception of a problem, our thinking and behaviour transform in the process.

The ability to reframe is the key skill involved in problem solving, and it requires a degree of self-confidence in order to 'let go' of the old habits of seeing and behaving. Without this minimal level of confidence, we are inclined to hold rigidly to the known as being the 'safer option' that poses the least threat. To someone with very little self-efficacy, reframing an event is stepping into the unknown and by its very nature this can induce anxiety. However, to 'not reframe' keeps us stuck in the same negative patterns of thinking and doing.

At the present time, Trevor is unable to reframe and he simply cannot visualise a different, better way of thinking and acting. The stress of his present situation and his perception of the pressures from the head teacher and the students fill him with disempowering anxiety, creating a depressed state. Without help, he is unable to adopt an alternative perspective on this situation. In his early years at the school, reframing had been one of Trevor's strengths and it had enabled him to move the school forward. Now Trevor's low self-esteem is draining him of the energy to adopt an alternative perspective (to reframe). Trevor needs to change the frame through which he perceives the head teacher's view of him (and his role in school) in order to change the meaning of the context from negative and hopeless to positive and hopeful. By doing this, his responses and behaviours will, in themselves, become more positive and energised.

Trevor may not be able to bring about such a radical change in his thinking without some form of support or professional intervention. The first step is recognition that there is a need for change: that his existing patterns of thought are cognitive distortions that are preventing him from feeling and being successful. Once he has this awareness, he will need the motivation to take appropriate action. There are innumerable books in the self-development genre, all suggesting different approaches to guide the individual towards personal transformation. Some approaches have their roots in cognitive or positive psychology, some are influenced by specific belief systems, and others are based on their authors' own specific journeys towards personal transformation. All resound with the same note of 'hope'. Many people claim that by reading and following the practices outlined in such books they have been helped to adopt more positive ways of thinking and acting. Others have found that they have needed additional guidance on their journey, getting such help from professionals – counsellors, coaches, therapists or mentors – or alternatively from other individuals within a support group setting.

---

### Ability to reframe: self-reflection exercise

Think of a particularly challenging problem that you have had to face. Now think about this same problem from the perspective of another person involved in it. How do the priorities change when you adopt this alternative viewpoint? Now try another perspective with different priorities on this same scenario. What do you notice from this vantage point?

Having distanced yourself in this way and tried on these alternative 'spectacles', go back to your starting point. Has your frame altered?

How could you use this process to help you deal more effectively with behavioural challenges in the classroom?

> Visualise yourself succeeding. Create a mental picture of
> yourself achieving your goals. Hold on to this picture
> tenaciously and never allow any thoughts of failure to
> intrude. Always picture success, no matter what prob-
> lems arise, keep the image sharp and it will guide you
> towards the reality.
>
> (Peale, 1996 [1953]: 17)

## Positive self-talk

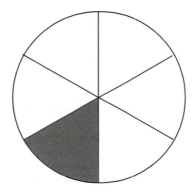

Self-efficacy requires an inner monologue that is positive and supportive of the self. As already stated, the first step in the process of
increasing one's self-efficacy requires the individual to become aware
of the character and tone of his/her 'inner voice'. For many individuals the initial stage of becoming aware of the inner voice's existence and power can be revelatory. Without awareness, individuals
cannot conceive of the power of their inner voice over their thought
patterns, self-beliefs and behaviour. Many people live their lives
without ever questioning the tremendous power of their internal
monologue, yet their lives are beset by self-imposed fears and anxieties, resulting in frustrations and unnecessary blockages to their
self-actualisation.

Personal development books and programmes that aim to help
individuals initiate change in some aspect or other of their lives are
predominantly based on the idea of 'reprogramming' the inner voice,
moving it away from negative habits of criticism to more supportive habits of nurturing and affirming the individual. This general
approach is grounded in a well-known cognitive therapy technique

in which individuals learn how to distinguish between realistic and maladaptive thinking patterns (Beck *et al.*, 2003). It is also reflected in certain psychotherapeutic practices (such as transactional analysis) that aim to undo the damage of negative self-beliefs held since early childhood.

Some writers (for example Louise Hay) advocate the use of positive affirmations to help individuals to change their internal realities. Making positive affirmations about one's abilities and powers is believed to help develop a strong, steady, growing self-confidence. According to Hay (1984), emotional difficulties arise out of a lack of self-love, and positive affirmations should therefore be used first to address this deficit. Other affirmations are then added as the individual grows in strength. The process of repeating affirmations has its origins in ancient Eastern meditation and other spiritual practices, and is seen as essential for the reprogramming of the unconscious mind. This could be thought of as a type of self-hypnosis, and it is often stated at the start of programmes that there is a need to repeat affirmations over and over in an almost mechanical way. Eventually affirmations may become incorporated into the individual's self-beliefs and it is at this point that there appears to be a marked shift in the individual's level of self-efficacy. It is also important to consider both the tone and the wording that are used. An empowering tone with a 'can do' message enables and energises the individual. Phrasing and careful choice of tense and words ensure that the individual's unconscious gets a clear message about the positive changes required so that these can be immediately put into action. When Norman Vincent Peale first began writing about the power of positive thinking in the 1950s, he stated that individuals need to affirm their own powers and abilities at least ten times every day, saying the affirmations in a strong, steady and confident manner. Peale stated that it was essential for individuals to believe in them and when facing difficult problems or barriers to repeat these affirmations over and over. This process was to prevent the old negative thoughts, beliefs and habits from regaining control.

Peale went on to advocate the use of positive quotations as a source of support to help drive out the old negative patterns. He suggested that such positive quotations could be carefully chosen: selected on the basis of creating feelings of courage and confidence for the individual. These should be repeated whenever the individual needs to fill his/her mind with thoughts of belief, confidence and security in order to push out all the old negative self-doubts.

If you or I or anybody think constantly of the forces that seem to be against us, we will build them up into a power far beyond that which is justified. They will assume a formidable strength, which they do not actually possess. But if, on the contrary, you mentally visualise and affirm and re-affirm your assets and keep your thoughts on them, emphasising them to the fullest extent, you will rise out of any difficulty regardless of what it may be.

(Peale, 1996 [1953]: 15)

Although this approach has attracted its fair share of critics and sceptics, there is a now growing body of scientific evidence that suggests that directed mental force (the power of the mind) can indeed lead to 'self-directed neuroplasticity' and observable changes in the wiring of the brain (Schwartz and Begley, 2002).

When Trevor began his teaching career he was positive in outlook, enthusiastic about his abilities as a teacher, open to new ideas and eager to share with colleagues and students. All this suggests that his inner voice was positive and supportive of himself during this period. This is now lacking, and Trevor is moving into a depressive state. If he does not recognise the impact of his mode of thinking on his abilities then he is engaging in an unconscious process of self-harm.

***Positive self-talk: self-reflection exercise***

Think about your own thinking processes (this is known as metacognition). Focus on yourself and your abilities. Try to do this in a detached way and note the tone, language or images that come to mind. Are they positive, supportive, praising and nurturing? Or are they critical, questioning, undermining and negative? Or are they a combination of the two?

Develop a hyper-awareness of your inner messages. Note when they are enabling and sustaining and work on increasing the frequency of these messages. Also note when your inner voice is critical and de-energising – why is this the case? What is the context that causes these negative messages to take hold? Is it possible through mental training to change the character of your inner voice to something more sustaining?

Do you celebrate each small step you take towards achieving your goals? Do you sustain your energy through a mental 'pat

on the back' whenever you complete a task giving you concern?
Do you use encouraging words to keep yourself going when
tired?

Do you periodically look back to see all that you have
achieved? In recent years? During your lifetime?

## Taking positive action

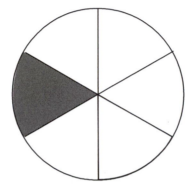

Once we are freed from self-doubt, self-efficacy is higher and we
become capable of taking positive action. This is the focus of the
fifth component of the self-efficacy domain. Taking positive action
is, in itself, integral to personal growth. It also serves as physical
feedback to the individual that he/she is having a positive impact on
the world, giving rise to increased feelings of self-worth. So taking
action is both an end result and part of the process (of increasing
self-efficacy) provided it is accompanied by the supportive inner
voice.

A high degree of self-efficacy enables teachers to feel appropriately
confident about their ability to create and maintain harmonious relationships in the classroom, and with this positive sense of self-belief
comes a higher level of energy. Teachers with low self-efficacy hold
on to the perception that their performance will be below what is
expected of them, and there will be an immediate 'leakage' of energy
and empowerment.

We experience this to varying degrees all of the time, although we
may not be conscious of the process. When we feel good about ourselves and confident in our abilities in a specific context, we are
empowered and energised to be active, take risks and be more creative.

When we are less sure about ourselves and our abilities, we lose energy, put off or avoid those tasks perceived as a challenge and confine ourselves to those aspects of our lives that we perceive as presenting little risk or challenge. We stick to what we see as safe and non-threatening.

Taking positive action helps in the building of self-efficacy but it also enables us to motivate, energise and support others in their own growth. This is particularly relevant to the classroom, where the teacher's personal belief in the successful outcome of the lesson translates into many positive behaviours that support the learning of the students. The teacher's positive determination to enable the student to grasp the specific element of understanding (the focus of the lesson) is presented in a learning context framed by the teacher's belief that the student can successfully achieve this goal. This is a potent element essential in a 'can do' culture.

At this point in his career, Trevor has never felt lower. He is losing his belief in himself as an effective teacher, which in turn is undermining his whole construct of himself in the world – that of being a natural teacher and skilful manager of behaviour. His lack of self-belief and increasing insecurity about his methods and style of teaching are beginning to immobilise Trevor. He is now finding that what used to be simple decisions for him, about what to do and how to do it, are taking an inordinate amount of his time both in lesson preparation and practically within the classroom. His hesitancy and lack of assertiveness in his dealings with the students are obviously having an impact on his ability to manage behaviour in the classroom.

---

### Taking positive action: self-reflection exercise

Are you aware of situations when you have failed to take positive action because you have been so preoccupied in thinking through all the possible outcomes to each possible course of action that you have simply given up without acting? Over-thinking can absorb more energy than simply doing and dealing with the consequences.

Can you think of a situation in which, with hindsight, you wish you had taken action sooner and where the outcome could have been better had there been earlier intervention and less time and energy spent on thinking through the pros and cons?

## Relishing challenge as an opportunity for growth

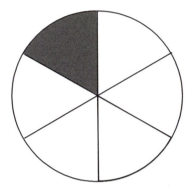

This is the final component of the pink domain, as it requires a high level of self-efficacy in order to see challenges or problems as something to be embraced. This comes as a result of seeing challenge as an opportunity for further growth and transformation. Linked with this component is the recognition that being alive means that one is constantly faced with challenge and opportunities for growth if one chooses. Relishing challenge means grasping the challenge in order to grow and transform rather than avoiding it or denying its existence.

Within the self-help genre there is general consensus that living bounded by fear prevents the individual from growing. In *Feel the Fear and Do It Anyway*, Susan Jeffers (1988) presents the limitations and frustrations of living bounded by fear as far more painful and damaging to the individual than the discomfort of pushing through the fear barrier. In her work and research on the negative impact of fear, she has observed that, once individuals have successfully pushed through a fear boundary, their sense of achievement and excitement at their own development and growth are such that other fear boundaries can be perceived as further opportunities for growth. Successfully pushing through this barrier enables individuals to see that fear has been a limiting factor in their life, preventing them from pursuing important goals and desires. The overcoming of fear (at whatever level) to achieve a goal can bring an immense sense of personal satisfaction and helps to enhance self-efficacy through mastery experience (Bandura, 1986). Relishing challenge as an opportunity to grow is recognition of this. It is the deliberate pushing back of the boundaries (fears, anxieties and limitations) that have kept us from fully exploring all that we are capable of.

We have seen that Trevor is at a very low point; his energy is diminishing, he is increasingly pessimistic about his abilities as a teacher and he is unable to adopt an alternative perspective on his situation. Trevor's low self-esteem is draining him of the motivation to take positive action. It could be argued that Trevor is bounded by fear of failure. He is afraid that he is not what he thought he was – a natural and effective teacher. Although he feels out of touch and left behind, he feels little inclination to attend training courses or even keep abreast of latest developments in education. This also reflects what Ross (1994) discovered, that low self-efficacy in teachers is linked to a reluctance to try new approaches and strategies. Trevor has talked himself into believing that it is not worth the effort.

Trevor has to find ways of stopping his negative inner messages, replacing them with a more positive, sustaining inner voice that will help him to find the energy and motivation necessary to take positive action. It is only when he is able to achieve this that Trevor will be in a position to see challenge as an opportunity for his personal growth.

---

### Relishing challenge as an opportunity for growth: self-reflection exercise

Think about an achievement that you are particularly proud of. Now think about the barrier you pushed through in order to attain this particular goal. Empathising with yourself prior to the successful outcome will remind you of the fear and anxiety that you experienced in the face of that challenge.

Do you perceive obstacles in your path as totally negative, to be got rid of as quickly as possible? Or do you perceive them as opportunities to learn?

Reflecting back on your own education (both formal and informal), think about those situations when you learned most effectively. Did they involve learning from your mistakes when trying to solve a real problem?

## A review of Trevor – adopting a 'whole-brain' approach

If Trevor had developed the cycle of components within the pink domain, the initial scenario might have looked more like this:

---

Trevor arrives at school on Monday morning with a determination to show the new head teacher that the judgements she seems to have formed about his practice are wrong. He is also determined to prove to himself that he is an outstanding practitioner; he knows he has both the energy and the ability (determination and will to change).

He has spent the weekend thinking long and hard about the head's feedback following last Thursday's lesson observation. Initially he focused on those aspects of his practice that she had criticised, which left him feeling defeated and de-energised. When he realised the impact this was having on his confidence and self-esteem, he quickly shifted his thinking to focus on positives about himself. He began by recalling what the head had praised about his teaching; then he moved on to what he knows he achieves in the classroom (eliminating negative self-talk).

Throughout the weekend, Trevor continued to build himself up by focusing on what his colleagues appreciate about him, what his students like and enjoy about his lessons, and what parents and other members of the school community value about his contribution to their school. In replaying all of this he was able to restore his shaken self-belief and find the necessary energy to plan for the forthcoming week (positive self-talk).

Over the weekend Trevor did a lot of careful thinking about his professional practice. Far from denying all of the head teacher's judgements, he accepted full **responsibility** for those aspects judged to be less than satisfactory. In his thinking he was able to empathise with the head teacher's perspective on the school, but particularly on his own classroom practice. This enabled him to view his performance in a new and different way (ability to reframe). With this insight in mind, together with his acceptance that changes were essential, Trevor spent a considerable amount of his weekend thinking about personal changes and seeking ways of addressing weaknesses in his practice (taking positive action).

Trevor enters the school with a renewed sense of what it is he is trying to achieve, both in the short term, in relation to his teaching on this particular Monday, and in the longer term, in what he wants to achieve both personally and professionally. Although last week had been very challenging, Trevor knows that it marked an important turning point for him which, with determination, will lead to his personal and professional growth and transformation.

*Table 11.1* Self-efficacy self-review

| What aspect of self-efficacy do I want to improve? | What can I do to improve this? | How will this impact on my management of behaviour? |
| --- | --- | --- |
|  |  |  |

# Chapter 12

# The whole is greater than the sum of its parts

> There are no things, only connections . . . only relationships.
>
> (Ferguson, 1980: 171)

Part I of this book mapped the development of ideas that shaped and informed our 'whole-brain' behaviour model. As described in Chapters 1–3, these ideas cross many discipline boundaries and encompass ancient wisdom through to cutting-edge research but, despite the diversity of their origins, their interconnectedness and compatibility are clearly intelligible. This idea of synergy, which is a central tenet of our model, opens up powerful new insights which can offer practitioners a more enduring philosophy on behaviour management, rather than relying on the collection of strategies and techniques that currently abound. We are not the first to comment on this exciting convergence of ideas. For example, Gerhardt (2004: 1) notes that 'Something new and exciting is happening . . . we have in fact arrived at a moment in which different disciplines are converging to produce a new understanding of emotional life.' We are suggesting, however, that this understanding could signal the way forward for behaviour management.

In this sense, it is our belief that the WBBM model can serve as a paradigm that encapsulates for the practitioner the *whole complexity* of the learning and teaching context. A distinguishing feature of the WBBM model is that it deliberately sets out not to simplify any element of the educational process. It draws attention to the infinite variables that constitute every human relationship and, in so doing, offers a framework in which these variables can be examined, understood and, where necessary, further developed through a process of personal transformation.

Throughout Part II of this book, we have examined the individual segments within the model in order to be able to explain the essential components of effective behaviour management to the practitioner. Analysis of each segment is necessary if the reader is to be able to understand and evaluate his/her own practice. For the 'whole' to be intact and the structure to be functional, the practitioner needs to be 'good enough' in each of the thirty-six components within the wheel of competencies. Because they are so interconnected, the structure is weakened if some of the components within segments are not addressed (imagine a peeled orange without the pith's connecting fibres that maintain the spherical whole).

With all the components in place and bound together by the interlacing of the key tools (responsibility, resilience, receptiveness and resolute optimism) and the stabilising axis of the core principles, the model creates its own synergy in which the combined effect becomes greater than the sum of its parts. This well-known saying has its roots in gestalt psychology, which embodies holistic principles and interprets phenomena as organised wholes rather than aggregates of distinct parts. As a school of thought, however, gestalt has struggled against the prevailing and accepted modes of research that have historically dominated academia and science and continue to do so today. Positivist influences still demand the study and analysis of physical phenomena through dissection or focus on a specific part or element, but frequently with scant reference to the whole or wider context. For centuries, scientific and academic research has been based on this narrow approach at the expense of achieving synthesis. With this absence of synthesis come fragmentation and the inherent dangers of lost perspective. Why does there need to be such a gap between the scientist and the humanist? Our model has been devised to help practitioners bridge this gap.

Even education has been characterised by the principles of focus, analysis and specialisation. This is understandable when we consider the thinking process when trying to learn or understand a new skill or field of knowledge. Systems have been built upon these early foundations resulting in increasingly specialised and specific ways of thinking that have become 'disciplines'. These disciplines each offer a particular way of comprehending the world and making sense of experience. In their philosophy of education, Hirst and Peters (1970) identified eight ways of knowing. These eight ways are neatly subsumed within our school systems of subjects, e.g. 'understanding and awareness of human behaviour' underpins the humanities.

As a result of this separation and specialisation, education has tended towards placing greater value on in-depth analysis rather than on synthesis and the ability to see patterns and connections. Education systems around the world have tended to produce gifted thinkers, highly skilled in specific, focused analytic thinking which is reflected in the type of research they conduct. However, these gifted individuals and groups place relatively little value (and therefore time) on looking for the connections with other disciplines or seeking the wider (contextual) implications and effects of the aspect they are studying. The shelves of most university libraries display a wealth of periodic journals each with their collection of esoteric research papers on subjects that have relatively minimal relevance to everyday living in our communities. Each month new and even more specialised journals come into being with research messages from narrower and narrower fields of study. These papers reflect the study and research of our brightest minds but sadly there is little evidence of much interdisciplinary connection. This in itself seems a mass of lost opportunities!

In striving to synthesise all the diverse elements that constitute effective practice, the WBBM model is, in effect, working in the opposite way. It may be necessary to analyse in order to identify specific patterns of behaviour but in carrying out this analysis we must not become blinkered and fail to see the complexity of the context in which adult and child are functioning. If, in trying to understand and resolve behaviour problems, we fail to take account of the 'whole' picture (be it the whole child, the whole relationship between teacher and student, or the whole context of the classroom, school or community), we are unlikely to achieve lasting success in our efforts. If we fail to recognise one another's wholeness then relational difficulties almost always arise.

In this way, our model was devised to be the antithesis of simplistic explanations for behaviour management and to provide a means of 'seeing' the whole. Its framework allows for the interconnections and the interrelatedness within and between contexts. It also has the capacity to acknowledge the dynamic and ever-changing nature of life (flow). We conceive of our model as being capable of encapsulating all the elements that a teacher needs to have sufficient mastery of in order to be able to provide effective behaviour management in the classroom.

As well as the connection with gestalt theory, this approach is also influenced by the general system theory (von Bertalanffy, 1968), which states that each variable in any system interacts with the other variables. In other words, cause and effect cannot be separated. This principle was first applied to the natural sciences by Bronfenbrenner (1979), who developed the theory in relation to human ecology and family therapy. Bronfenbrenner described how everything in a child's environment affects the way that he/she develops and it may be necessary therefore to direct the intervention at particular sub-systems such as the family or the teacher. A systems approach therefore acknowledges that problem behaviour is not simply something that belongs to the student but is the product of interactions and relationships.

The thinking behind humanity's greatest innovations has never been simply linear and logical. Creativity within any field requires a leap of the imagination to make the novel connection, giving rise to the original idea. Although personal accounts of the 'eureka' moment suggest that the creative insight just 'appears', seemingly from nowhere, further analysis suggests that at an unconscious level the brain has been working in an interconnected way, synthesising knowledge and understanding in a way that would be impossible consciously. Gestalt theorists argue that, when viewing the 'whole', the mind necessarily makes a leap from comprehending the parts to realising the whole. It is for this reason that we have sought to make connections and synthesise. As humans, functioning with our whole brains, as opposed to limiting our thinking along particular narrow pathways, enables us to synthesise innumerable divergent ideas. By this means, 'whole-brain' thinking allows us to be innovative and creative in our thinking, our problem solving and more generally the way we live our lives. From our own experience, this process of 'whole-brain' thinking has been enormously rewarding, and the growing capacity to see patterns and make connections enabled us to grow and transform not only as teachers but also as human beings.

# Epilogue

Only connect! . . . Live in fragments no longer.

(E.M. Forster, 1910: 174)

E.M. Forster was not only a great writer but also a secular humanist. In his novel *Howards End*, the famous dictum 'Only connect!' carries two meanings. One is a call to unite the opposing elements of reason and emotion that coexist within each of us (what the character Margaret Schlegel calls 'the beast and the monk' and 'the prose and the passion'). The other meaning is a call for us to invest more time and energy into understanding others in order to develop more harmonious interpersonal relationships.

E.M. Forster demonstrates, through his literary characters, how human beings too often fail to perceive the connections that link them to other people and to events that are beyond their immediate sphere. This includes the seen or physical as well as the unseen or spiritual influences. This is the essence of what we have tried to communicate through our model: that in establishing these connections, teachers may be better able to identify their missing pieces and see the whole picture!

> . . . there was one quality in Henry for which she was never prepared, however much she reminded herself of it: his obtuseness. He simply did not notice things, and there was no more to be said. He never noticed that Helen and Frieda were hostile . . . he never noticed the lights and shades that exist in the greyest conversation, the finger-posts, the milestones, the collisions, the illimitable views. Once – on another occasion – she scolded him about it. He was puzzled, but replied with a laugh: 'My motto is

concentrate. I've no intention of frittering away my strength on that sort of thing.' 'It isn't frittering away the strength,' she protested. 'It's enlarging the space in which you may be strong.'

(Forster, 1910: 175)

# Appendix: CAB key and profile sheet

## Organisation

Time management is one of my strengths (13).

I am efficient at managing paperwork and record keeping (25).

I usually arrive in good time for lessons, appointments and meetings (3).

I'm known as the one who carries spare tissues/pens/meeting documents/cash, etc. just in case . . . (41).

I'm the sort of person that likes to plan things well ahead (19).

It is important to me to have a place for everything and everything in its place (49).

I'm the sort of person who likes to know exactly what to expect when faced with new or unfamiliar situations (8).

Structure and routines are important to me (16).

I can't bear mess (30).

## Self-efficacy

I usually look on the bright side of life (5).

I always make a point of learning from my mistakes rather than feeling defeated or knocked back by them (11).

I seek out and embrace new ideas and exciting challenges (37).

I know what I'm good at and I build on my strengths (47).

I am good at finding my own solutions to any worries or problems that I face (9).

I normally bounce back quickly after a disappointment (15).

I am not easily intimidated by people or challenging situations (26).

I believe that people make their own luck in this world (18).

I know I have the potential to succeed in the things I want to achieve (32).

## Emotional literacy

I seem to know instinctively how others are feeling (2).
I almost always keep calm in difficult situations (24).
I usually stop and think before I speak my mind (46).
When I get angry, I am unlikely to swear or start crying (52).
I always try to consider the other person's point of view whenever there is a conflict of views, wants or needs (27).
I handle myself well during arguments and can usually reach a compromise (6).
I am good at calming people down or cheering them up (29).
I rarely sulk or storm off when someone upsets me (42).
I can accept compliments and positive feedback without embarrassment or dismissal (33).

## Knowledge

I always try to read and keep up with current ideas in education (28).
I get enormous satisfaction from passing on knowledge to others (34).
I get a real buzz from sharing new ideas and things I have learned (17).
It is a priority of mine to learn new things and try to expand my knowledge (53).
I go to conferences and lectures whenever possible – to keep up with developments in my field(s) of interest (40).
I'm the kind of person who will ask lots of questions if I don't know something (1).
I will often seek advice from other people or books in order to make a better job of things even if this means delaying a task (7).
I am known to have an enthusiastic interest in certain subjects (arts/science/history/music, etc.) (43).
I like to read up about places before I visit them (22).

## Communication

I am often conscious of body language (both my own and other people's) (44).
People often confide in me or tell me that I'm a good listener (10).
I hardly ever shout or raise my voice unnecessarily (36).
I am able to say 'no' to people without losing their respect (50).
I reckon people would describe me as 'good company' (38).

I think people would describe me as very courteous and polite (12).

I can express my needs without being overly apologetic or awkward about it (48).

I tend to get elected as a spokesperson (4).

I'm a mediator and good at resolving arguments between other people (21).

## Psychology

It is important for me to understand the underlying reasons for a particular or 'challenging' behaviour (35).

I try to make sense of and analyse my own behaviour (14).

I often find myself puzzling over why someone is behaving in a particular way (45).

I am fascinated by human relationships and I enjoy films and novels that explore this dimension (31).

I am intrigued by what makes people tick (39).

I understand the difference between behaviourist and cognitive approaches to behaviour management (23).

I continuously monitor and assess the effectiveness of the rewards and sanctions that I use in the classroom (54).

I'm interested in psychological theory (20).

I can think of several approaches and classroom strategies that are influenced by a humanistic perspective on behaviour (51).

*Figure A.1* Profile of WBBM competencies.

The chart shows six competency categories, each represented as a column divided into nine rows:

| Organisation | Self-efficacy | Emotional literacy | Knowledge | Communication | Psychology |
|---|---|---|---|---|---|

# Notes

## 1  Opening the box

1 This quotation is attributed (without a source text) to Maslow by Ornstein (1986: 60).
2 Kelly's personal construct theory (1955).
3 Brand name for methylphenidate, a drug prescribed for individuals with attention deficit hyperactivity disorder.
4 Refers to the growing trend in the UK of banning the wearing of hooded tops in shopping malls, restaurants and other public places.
5 Anti-social behaviour orders were introduced in the UK in 1999 under the provisions of the Crime and Disorder Act 1998.

## 2  Laying the pieces out

1 Functional magnetic resonance imaging.

# References

Abramson, L.Y., Seligman, M.E.P. and Teasdale, J.D. (1978). Learned helplessness in humans: critique and reformulation. *Journal of Abnormal Psychology*, 87: 49–74.

Argyris, C. (1976). *Increasing Leadership Effectiveness*. New York: Wiley.

Ashton, P.T. and Webb, R.B. (1986). *Making a Difference: Teachers' Sense of Efficacy and Student Achievement*. New York: Longman.

Austin, J.H. (2006). *Zen-Brain Reflections*. Cambridge, MA: MIT Press.

Bandler, R. and Grinder, J. (1979). *Frogs into Princes*. Moab, UT: Real People Press.

Bandler, R. and Grinder, J. (1981). *Reframing: Neuro-linguistic Programming and the Transformation of Meaning*. Moab, UT: Real People Press.

Bandura, A. (1977). Self-efficacy: toward a unifying theory of behaviour change. *Psychological Review*, 84: 191–215.

Bandura, A. (1986). *Social Foundations of Thought and Action: A Social Cognitive Theory*. Englewood Cliffs, NJ: Prentice-Hall.

Barrow, G. and Newton, T. (eds) (2004). *Walking the Talk: How Transactional Analysis Is Improving Behaviour and Raising Self-Esteem*. London: David Fulton.

Beck, A.T., Freeman, A. and Davis, D.D. (2003). *Cognitive Therapy of Personality Disorders*. New York: Guilford Press.

Bennathan, M. and Boxall, M. (1996). *Effective Intervention in Primary Schools: Nurture Groups*, 2nd edn. London: David Fulton.

Berg, Y. (2003). *The Power of Kabbalah*. London: Hodder & Stoughton.

Berne, E. (1961). *Transactional Analysis in Psychotherapy*. New York: Grove Press (reprinted 1975, London: Souvenir Press).

Bertalanffy, L. von (1968). *General System Theory*. New York: Brazillier.

Betz, N.E. and Hackett, G. (1981). The relationship of career-related self-efficacy expectations to perceived career options in college women and men. *Journal of Counselling Psychology*, 28: 399–410.

Bocchino, R. (1999). *Emotional Literacy: To Be a Different Kind of Smart*. London: Sage.

Bronfenbrenner, U. (1979). *The Ecology of Human Development*. Cambridge, MA: Harvard University Press.

Bruer, J.T. (1997). Education and the brain: a bridge too far. *Educational Researcher*, 26(8): 4–16.

Bruer, J.T. (1999). *Schools for Thought*. Boston, MA: MIT Press.

Canter, L. and Canter, M. (1992). *Assertive Discipline*. Bristol: Behaviour Management.

Chopra, D. (1989). *Quantum Healing*. New York: Bantam Books.

Coffield, F., Moseley, D., Hall, E. and Ecclestone, K. (2004). *Learning Styles and Pedagogy in Post–16 Learning: A Systematic and Critical Review*. London: Learning and Skills Research Centre.

Coladarci, T. (1992). Teachers' sense of efficacy and commitment to teaching. *Journal of Experimental Education*, 60: 323–337.

Croll, P. and Moses, D. (1985). *One in Five: The Assessment and Incidence of Special Educational Needs*. London: Routledge & Kegan Paul.

Damasio, A. (1994). *Descartes' Error: Emotion, Reason, and the Human Brain*. London: Pan Macmillan.

Damasio, A. (1999). *The Feeling of What Happens: Body and Emotion in the Making of Consciousness*. New York: Harcourt Brace.

Damasio, A. (2003). *Looking for Spinoza: Joy, Sorrow and the Feeling Brain*. New York: Harcourt Brace.

Davidson, R.J., Kabat-Zinn, J., Schumacher, J., Rosenkranz, M., Muller, D., Santorelli, S.F., Urbanowski, F., Harrington, A., Bonus, K. and Sheridan, J.F. (2003). Alterations in brain and immune function produced by mindfulness meditation. *Psychosomatic Medicine*, 65: 564–570.

Derrington, C. and Groom, B. (2004). *A Team Approach to Behaviour Management*. London: Paul Chapman.

Dewey, J. (1916). *How We Think: A Restatement of the Relation of Reflective Thinking to the Education Process*. Chicago, IL: Henry Regnery.

Dimmick, S. (1995). *Successful Communication through NLP*. Aldershot: Gower.

Eriksson, P.S., Perfilieva, E., Bjork-Eriksson, T., Alborn, A.M., Nordborg, C., Peterson, D.A. and Gage, F.H. (1998). Neurogenesis in the adult human hippocampus. *Nature Medicine*, 4(11): 1313–1317.

Evans, J., Harden, A., Thomas, J. and Benefield, P. (2003). Support for pupils with emotional and behavioural difficulties (EBD) in mainstream primary classrooms: a systematic review of the effectiveness of interventions. In *Research Evidence in Education Library*. London: EPPI-Centre, Social Science Research Unit, Institute of Education.

Ferguson, M. (1980). *The Aquarian Conspiracy: Personal and Social Transformation in Our Time*. New York: Tarcher Penguin.

Ferguson, M. (2002). *The Aquarian Conspiracy*, rev. edn. New York: Tarcher Penguin.

Fisher, E.A. and Sharp, S.W. (2004). *The Art of Managing Everyday Conflict: Understanding Emotions and Power Struggles*. Westport, CT: Praeger.

Flavell, J.H. (1976). Metacognitive aspects of problem solving. In L.B. Resnick (ed.), *The Nature of Intelligence*, pp. 231–235. Hillsdale, NJ: Erlbaum.

Forster, E.M. (1910, reprinted 1941). *Howards End*. Harmondsworth: Penguin.

Fox, B.B. (1991). Teachers' opinions of assertive discipline. *Education in Review*, 9: 12–19.

Freire, P. (1996). *Letters to Christina: Reflections on My Life and Work*. London: Routledge.

Gardner, H. (1983). *Frames of Mind: The Theory of Multiple Intelligences*. New York: Basic Books.

Gardner, H. (1993). *Multiple Intelligences: The Theory in Practice*. New York: Basic Books.

Geake, J. (2005). Developmental neuroscience: directions and implications for educational research – discussant comments. Brain, Education and Neuroscience SIG, AERA, Montreal.

George, M. (2003). *The 7 Aha!s of Highly Enlightened Souls*. Winchester: O Books.

Gerhardt, S. (2004). *Why Love Matters: How Affection Shapes a Baby's Brain*. London: Routledge.

Giallo, R. and Little, E. (2003). Classroom behaviour problems: the relationship between preparedness, classroom experiences and self-efficacy in graduate and student teachers. *Australian Journal of Educational and Developmental Psychology*, 3: 21–34.

Gold, R., Evans, N. and Coleman, D. (2005). *Running a School 2004/5: Legal Duties and Responsibilities*. Bristol: Jordan Publishing.

Goleman, D. (1996). *Emotional Intelligence: Why It Can Matter More than IQ*. London: Bloomsbury.

Goleman, D. (ed.) (1997). *Healing Emotions: Conversations with the Dalai Lama on Mindfulness, Emotions and Health*. Boston, MA: Shambhala.

Goleman, D. (2006). *Social Intelligence: The New Science of Human Relationships*. New York: Bantam Books.

Goswami, U. (2004). Neuroscience and education. *British Journal of Educational Psychology*, 74: 1–14.

Hall, J. (2005). *Neuroscience and Education: A Review of the Contribution of Brain Science to Teaching and Learning*, SCRE Research Report 121. Glasgow: Scottish Council for Research in Education.

Hargreaves, D. (2005). *About Learning: Report of the Learning Working Group*. London: Demos.

Hay, L. (1984). *You Can Heal Your Life*. London: Eden Grove Publications.

Heider, F. (1958). *The Psychology of Interpersonal Relationships*. New York: Wiley.

Herrmann, N. (1990). *The Creative Brain*. Lake Lure, NC: Ned Herrmann Group.

Hirst, P.H. and Peters, R.S. (1970). *The Logic of Education*. London: Routledge & Kegan Paul.

James, W. (2005 [1899]). *Talks to Teachers on Psychology; and to Students on Some of Life's Ideals*. Boston, MA: IndyPublish.com.

Jeffers, S. (1988). *Feel the Fear and Do It Anyway*. New York: Ballantine Books.

Joyce, J. and Showers, B. (2006 [1995]). In L. Browne, Proposing a proximal principle between peer coaching and staff development as a driver for transformation. *International Journal of Evidence Based Coaching and Mentoring*, 4(1): 31–44.

Jung, C.G. (1933). *Modern Man in Search of a Soul*. London: Kegan Paul Trench Trubner.

Kelley, H.H. (1967). Attribution theory in social psychology. In D. Levine (ed.), *Nebraska Symposium on Motivation*, vol. 15, pp. 129–238. Lincoln: University of Nebraska Press.

Kelly, G.A. (1955). *The Psychology of Personal Constructs*, vols 1 and 2. New York: Norton.

Kounin, J.S. (1970). *Discipline and Group Management in Classrooms*. New York: Holt, Rinehart and Winston.

Kuhn, T.S. (1962). *The Structure of Scientific Revolutions*. Chicago, IL: University of Chicago Press.

McCrone, J. (1999). 'Right brain' or 'left brain' myth or reality? *New Scientist*, 2193: 26–30.

Macgrath, M. (2000). *The Art of Peaceful Teaching in the Primary School*. London: David Fulton.

MacLean, P. (1973). *A Triune Concept of the Brain and Behaviour*. Toronto: University of Toronto Press.

Maguire, E.A., Gadian, D.S., Johnsrude, I.S., Good, C.D., Ashburner, J., Frackowiak, R.S. and Frith, C.D. (2000). Navigation related structural change in the hippocampi of taxi drivers. *Proceedings of the National Academy of Sciences of the United States of America*, 97: 4398–4403.

Margo, J. and Dixon, M., with Pearce, N. and Reed, H. (2006). *Freedom's Orphans: Raising Youth in a Changing World*. London: Institute for Public Policy Research (IPPR).

Maslow, A.H. (1968). *Toward a Psychology of Being*. New York: John Wiley & Sons.

Matthews, B. (2006). *Engaging Education: Developing Emotional Literacy, Equity and Co-education*. Maidenhead: Open University Press.

Miller, A., Ferguson, E. and Byrne, I. (2000). Pupils' causal attributions for difficult classroom behaviour. *British Journal of Educational Psychology*, 70: 85–96.

Mortiboys, A. (2005). *Teaching with Emotional Intelligence*. Abingdon: Routledge.

OECD (2002). *Understanding the Brain: Towards a New Learning Science*. Paris: Organisation for Economic Co-operation and Development.

Ornstein, R. (1986). *The Psychology of Consciousness*, 2nd rev. edn. London: Penguin.

Panksepp, J. (1998). *Affective Neuroscience: The Foundations of Human and Animal Emotions*. Oxford: Oxford University Press.

Peale, N.V. (1996 [1953]). *The Power of Positive Thinking*, reissue edn. New York: Ballantine Books.

Redfield, J. and Adrienne, C. (1995). *The Celestine Prophecy: An Experiential Guide*. London: Bantam Books.

Rizzollatti, G. and Craighero, L. (2004). The mirror-neuron system. *Annual Review of Neuroscience*, 29: 169–192.

Robertson, I.H. (1999). *Mind Sculpture: Unlocking Your Brain's Untapped Potential*. New York: Fromm International.

Rogers, J. (2004). *Coaching Skills: A Handbook*. Maidenhead: Open University Press.

Rogers, W. (1992). *Managing Teacher Stress*. London: Pitman Publishing.

Rogers, W. (1998). *You Know the Fair Rule*, 2nd edn. London: Prentice Hall.

Rosengren, K.E. (2000). *Communication*. London: Sage.

Ross, J.A. (1994). Beliefs that make a difference: the origins and impacts of teacher efficacy. Paper presented at the annual meeting of the Canadian Association for Curriculum Studies.

Rotter, J.B. (1966). Generalized expectancies for internal versus external control of reinforcement. *Psychological Monographs*, 80: 1–28.

Ryan, K. and Oestreich, D. (1991). Driving fear out of the workplace. In M. Macgrath (2000). *The Art of Peaceful Teaching in the Primary School*. London: David Fulton.

Salovey, P. and Mayer, J.D. (1990). Emotional intelligence. *Imagination, Cognition, and Personality*, 9: 185–211.

Schwartz, J.M. and Begley, S. (2002). *The Mind and the Brain: Neuroplasticity and the Power of Mental Force*. New York: HarperCollins.

Seligman, M. (1998). *Learned Optimism: How to Change Your Mind and Your Life*. London: Pocket Books.

Seligman, M.E.P. and Czikszentmihalyi, M. (2000). Positive psychology: an introduction. *American Psychologist*, 55(1): 5–14.

Sharp, P. (2001). *Nurturing Emotional Literacy*. London: David Fulton.

Starr, J. (2003). *The Coaching Manual*. Harlow: Pearson Education.

Steiner, C. (1981). *The Other Side of Power*. New York: Grove Press.

Steiner, C. (2002). *Emotional Literacy: Intelligence with a Heart*, www.emotional-literacy.com.

Sunderland. M. (2000). *Helping Children with Feelings*. Bicester: Speech Marks Publications.

Taylor, M.J. (2003). *Going Round in Circles: Implementing and Learning from Circle Time*. Slough: NFER.

Terman, L.M. (1938). *Psychological Factors in Marital Happiness*. New York: McGraw-Hill.

Thorndike, E.L. (1920). Intelligence and its uses. *Harper's Magazine*, 140: 227–235.

Tschannen-Moran, M. and Woolfolk Hoy, A. (2001). Teacher efficacy: capturing an elusive construct. *Teaching and Teacher Education*, 17: 783–805.

Vingerhoets, G., Berckmoes, C. and Stroobant, N. (2003). Cerebral hemodynamics during discrimination of prosodic and semantic emotion in speech studied by transcranial doppler ultrasonography. *Neuropsychology*, 17(1): 93–99.

Watson, J.B. (1928). *Psychological Care of Infant and Child*. New York: W.W. Norton.

Weare, K. (2004). *Developing the Emotionally Literate School*. London: Paul Chapman.

Whitebread, D. (2002). The implications for early years education of current research in cognitive neuroscience. Paper presented at the Annual Conference of the British Educational Research Association, University of Exeter, 12–14 September, www.leeds.ac.uk/educol/documents/00002545.htm (accessed 31 January 2007).

Whitworth, L., Kimsey-House, H. and Sandahl, P. (1998). *Co-active Coaching: New Skills for Coaching People for Success in Work and Life*. Mountain View, CA: Davies-Black Publishing.

Yearley, L. (1997). Three views of virtue. In D. Goleman (ed.), *Healing Emotions*. Boston, MA: Shambhala.

Zull, J.E. (2002). *The Art of Changing the Brain: Enriching the Practice of Teaching by Exploring the Biology of Learning*. Sterling, VA: Stylus.

# Index